A Customer Centric Approach to
Creating a Customer for Life.

Effective Customer Success Execution

Jackie Golden

This book is dedicated to my loving husband, Jerry Golden, who has been my best friend, supporter of my career and mentor for the last 35 years. I would not be who I am today without him as my life long partner.

FOREWORD

I grew up as the son of a software entrepreneur.

My father would share with me wisdom from his experience in the working world. One of his favorite things to say was "Son, in business you're either building the product or selling it." But after spending the last 17 years building technology companies of my own, I now understand that today's economy is radically different from the one in which my father operated.

You see, today, your success as a business is inextricably linked to the success of your customers. This goes far beyond building and selling product -- if your customers aren't realizing radical value from your products or services, renewing their contracts, referring you to other customers, etc., your bottom line as a company is at risk.

We spend a lot of time at Gainsight helping evangelize this message to the world. We call this new mindset of orienting around the customer, Customer Success. This isn't just a clever buzzword tied to rhetoric, but a full-fledged business practice that the leading companies in the world are employing to drive revenue.

One of the key tenants of Customer Success is to align all customer touch points around a well-executed customer experience model as a means of growing your installed base of loyal customers. Although great "customer service" has been a hot discussion topic over the last 10 years, the idea of building the ultimate customer experience goes further to involve every functional area of the company.

Jackie's approach to building a Customer Life Cycle model as the heart of a company's customer experience framework is powerful for companies to build customers for life with consistency and quality. It will give your company a competitive edge and the ability to drive innovation and thought leadership capabilities within your teams. Her passion for creating the kind of success for customers that is truly indispensable to how the company operates is infectious. She challenges you to really understand the customer's perception of how effective your product is in providing improved operational effectiveness, innovation capabilities or driving revenue and growth. My favorite quote is *"The customer's perception is my reality."*

I have read many great business books over the years and what I love about this book is that it is an excellent implementation guide for building the foundational elements that create a strong basis for the organizations to work together better with the customer experience as the focus. Jackie shares her secrets for how she has helped some of the top software companies find tremendous success and high growth profitably by using this customer experience framework as the center of her strategy.

I believe that if more companies embrace this approach to their go-to market strategies, they would find this to be a shorter pathway to attaining healthy (and sustainable) growth. The rich content Jackie shares with a logical and easy to follow implementation methodology will provide many organizations a great way to build their customer experience models that will work.

As more businesses are embracing a subscription-based pricing model, investing in Customer Success (early) is no longer an optional exercise. Your customers are your company's growth engine. With the principles Jackie describes in *Effective Customer Success Execution*, you've now got the definitive playbook for delivering an end-to-end customer experience focused on driving unparalleled degrees of success for your customers, and therefore, to your company.

I'll be sure to send my father a copy.

Nick Mehta, CEO
Gainsight

INTRODUCTION

"Customer experience," or CX, has become a hot topic in the past decade. This guide will show you how to build a world-class customer experience model that delivers a results-driven approach that ensures a consistent, repeatable, and quality customer experience for your clients over the long term.

As an executive with 30 years' corporate experience and 20 years in high tech, I have helped dozens of companies develop a successful customer experience model. This book builds on those results to share proven strategies that work. This model has been developed over the last 20 years from my experience building a customer experience approach in the high tech industry for companies like Hyperion, Cognos, Ascential, IBM, and Workfront (formerly AtTask). I have optimized the model over time by targeting works in order to build the best results-driven customer experience model.

In short, the most successful customer experience model generates an increase in sales and long-term customer fans in a profitable way. The model I have found successful and executed at WorkFront created a consistent approach to selling and servicing customers that increased sales, created a profitable services organization, improved renewal rates, and provided an increase in expansion opportunities. I have continued to work with high growth, high tech companies and help them build a customer experience model with the right strategies using precise execution plans, built on proven models that provides their customers with the right customer experience to hook them and keep them.

TABLE OF CONTENTS

CHAPTER ONE

The Benefits of a Customer focused business model and strategy

Over the last 20 years, I have had the pleasure of working with hundreds of customers, specifically in the high tech industry, helping them implement software solutions that were designed to revolutionize their business and to provide a competitive edge.

As many of you have probably experienced, thoughtful and strategic use of technology provides a significant edge to innovation capabilities, operational effectiveness, automation, employee capacity and productivity, and many more operational improvements.

Many great technology companies have helped transform top corporations worldwide with their hardware, software and various product innovations. Most of these innovations have focused on improving specific aspects of a corporation. For example, financial reporting with improved transparencies and insights. In addition, there was the business intelligence craze, which offered dashboard reporting on key Performance Indicators (KPIs).

Then we had the ERP revelation in automating manufacturing and tracking more insightful information to find ways to reduce costs. Remember, too, the Master Data Management era that uncovered the power of quality data versus bad data and how to maintain "one source of the truth". Of course, my favorite is the latest around Big Data Analytics and the ability for technology to actually learn from the data and provide answers and predictions.

Wait! What happened to the customer experience? Notice that in all these innovations to help companies succeed and grow, the focus was never really about what the customer was experiencing as part of the strategic formula for success. It was a combination of behavior management techniques, with a solid strategic plan, that created the right corporate climate, which followed a concise dashboard of key metrics and targets, with the right people on the bus who were motivated in the right ways, creating an excellent quality product. Finally, there was the idea of a solid customer support team. However, a customer success program or the development of all of the above elements lacked a focus on the customer's expectations and the value required to be a transformative solution for the customer.

Only in the last five to ten years has the concept of creating a customer success plan become critical in creating a successful company.

By contrast, when I left the corporate finance world and joined my first technology company, Hyperion, as a consultant, my focus right from the beginning was listening to what the customer was trying to accomplish and finding the best solution for them using the Hyperion products.

Ultimately I created my own methodology, which became my personal approach to consulting with each customer to whom I was assigned. In fact, Hyperion created a methodology shortly after I joined. And I was able to contribute to the final outcome. However, I was one of the few people in the meetings who kept mentioning that our focus should be to create a better solution for the customer. I thought we should focus on what would make the most impactful financial solution besides just the basic reporting.

The Hyperion methodology team was focused on creating a best practice approach with a prescriptive step by step set of tasks that all consultants should follow and documents that were required to be delivered on each assignment. As Hyperion evolved into a larger company with multiple products, the methodology began to crack because we didn't have a best practice approach to designing a robust, impactful end-to-end solution using all of our products so that the customer would receive a clear vision of the final solution with a detailed roadmap of how to get from where they were to the ultimate vision.

Don't get me wrong, I have also worked with customers that had no idea where to start or even what they wanted. They knew only that there had to be a better way and they heard that Hyperion was a great product. In those cases, of course, we had to create a plan and provide a roadmap for them. But the real difference was that I helped them define the vision and a clear roadmap on how to get from where they were to the vision. I was also determined to transfer my knowledge and experience to them so they could begin to see how the technology could provide them with the solutions that helped transform their business.

It then turned into a more collaborative conversation over time so that the customers were able to create better ways, new designs, reports and types of information that would enable them to do their job better and to provide the company with more insightful reports. That's when it was fun and exciting. The student became the teacher and I began to learn from them. It added to my knowledge and abilities to deliver a more tailored solution to meet my customer's needs based on their type of business and industry in my future consulting.

So why do I share this story with you? It is the lessons of these stories and the success that followed that empowered me to create the Customer Experience framework and a new, innovative approach that helps companies develop the best Customer Success strategy that will drive the outcomes and results that shoot them to the top of their market.

In my last few years with Hyperion, I was in the Strategic Account Management group with a focus on the large strategic accounts like CoBank, Phelps Dodge, Safeway, and many others. Our team mission was to manage multiple implementations of the Hyperion products across many customer teams and organizations. Again, I found myself asking the executive sponsors at these accounts a lot of "Why" type questions. It was vital to understand their business model, how they do business, why were they looking for this type of solution, and what they expected the solution to do for the company. In other words, only after we understood what they defined as their success criteria could we determine what we had to deliver. By delivering to their success criteria, we were developing a loyal relationship so that they would walk into their next executive or leadership meeting and rave about our solution that would optimize their results.

I'll never forget my first "Whiteboard" session at CoBank in Colorado. I had representatives from all the organizations that were interested in using the Hyperion products in the same room. Although they were looking to me right away for all the answers, they ended up spending the first few hours answering questions. As they answered my questions about their business, I began to draw a model of how they were organized and how they operated including how data flowed so we could discover the best source of information that we needed to integrate into the Hyperion products. We also ended up with some nice diagrams of how they operated today that mapped out their processes and interactions with other groups. It showed many bottlenecks, duplicate information, and conflicts, which was interesting to many of the team members who were unaware of these issues.

The surprise came when the team members began asking each other more about the diagrams on the board. They began to edit my drawings and create their version of reality. But they didn't all agree. In fact, many team members were surprised by the information and were learning more about how their own company actually operated. This discovery process helped the team to agree on where they were today and what the priorities should be for a Phase I solution to provide the most impactful benefits to the company. Want to guess how close it was to what was originally discovered in the sales cycle? Nowhere near what the team had defined as their success criteria during the sales cycle.

This process became a running theme from customer to customer. I did the same thing at Phelps Dodge and Safeway. The sales team was fascinated by the results of these "Whiteboard" sessions and how much they drove the real plan and strategy we put in place for deploying the Hyperion products and the final solution that the customer's implemented. This triggered the Sales Organization to create a Strategy Workshop where they brought in the Strategic Account Managers to help map these strategies and key success factors upfront. By setting the expectations correctly upfront in the sales cycle and by developing the right services program to ensure success, we were able to improve our "Time to Value" metric during the implementation stage of the customer's experience with Hyperion. It also enabled an expansion opportunity to come to fruition in a shorter time frame. Sales would then use this metric and the customer stories as references in their future sales cycles.

This real-life story illustrates how the focus on the customer's success with our solution drove more than just the implementation strategy or methodology. It also drove changes in the sales approach and eventually the product roadmap. The residual effect was that these customer's were all top references for us. One of the best compliments these customers would say about us was: *"Your team listens to our problems and difficulties and helps us strategize the best way to solve these problems with your solution."* They saw us as a team, not just a sales guy selling a product and tossing it to a consultant to implement something that may or may not work for them. They achieved the benefits of the teams working together with the best interests of the customer in mind.

An intense customer focus from the sales and services implementation and support teams provides a powerful first impact the customer experiences with your company in addition to the marketing events that draw them in as a prospect. As we all know, you must actually deliver on the promises that you market and sell. In other words, set expectations correctly and then deliver on them so that the customer believes that they have received every bit of the value you sold them. So what role do your other company organizations play in the customer's experience to optimize the customer's long-term relationship with your company?

Other organizations in your company have plenty of opportunities to improve the customer's experience and the perception of your company, its products, and services.

The Marketing organization is an obvious example. They create the look and feel of the company and the products via all the social and physical media available today. This is often the first experience the customer has with your company. Marketing can quickly make or break a customer's interest in your company. This is primarily associated with how easy it was to understand quickly who you are, what you offer, and how can you help them solve critical or high priority problems.

Typically customers go looking for technology to solve a problem that is big enough to warrant a serious search for a solution. In some cases, you may have a product that solves a problem they don't know they have. In those cases, you must make it easy for them to quickly understand how they benefit from what you solve and how you solve it. The experience you are trying to create in this case is to intrigue them enough to contact you for more information.

In both of these scenarios you create a customer experience that enables them to form a positive opinion about your company and product. In previous work lives with Cognos, Ascential, IBM, and WorkFront, I spent time each quarter doing customer tours within each region worldwide. After creating a list of customers that represented each of our target markets and different company sizes, I would schedule a quarterly tour. During the tours I would typically learn about their experience with our marketing, sales, consulting, education, support, and customer success programs.

During one of these tours with Cognos, I was presenting our Corporate Performance Management solution at Cognos to a new prospect with the sales team. I had incorporated a mini whiteboard session into my presentation and had created some drawings of the vision on the board to get consensus from the team. When I was done and asked the team if they felt this was the right solution and vision for their company, the CFO said, *"You should put that drawing on your website and tell the story just like that. The marketing webinar and website make it sound like your business intelligence solution and budgeting and forecasting solution are two different solutions. You made it all come together for us."* For the CFO that drawing was the hook. Many marketing tactics can be great hooks, but the test is: Do the prospects and current customers perceive the information the way you think they do?

How many marketing departments take their marketing materials and campaigns out to current customers and ask the question: *"What is your perception of this new campaign, these materials or this presentation?"* It is always valuable to get a perspective from a cross section of new prospects that has never heard of you or your products along with current customers who know you. You might find some messages and images provide the right perception and are easily consumed right off to both audiences or that one audience gets it more easily than another.

As a leader in these high tech companies, I have learned the genuine value of supporting a customer experience as part of an end-to-end Customer Life Cycle model. As I describe in detail later in the book, this approach requires every organization within a company to play a role in bringing a new customer on board and in providing vital information to support them long term.

In any customer's life cycle journey with your company, one of the key processes customers have to complete with your company is the actual business transaction. The main organization involved in executing and supporting the business transactions is the Finance team that usually has an accounting, finance, and legal group. Sometimes, we don't think about the customer's interaction with these Finance folks when they decide to buy and continue to buy from you. However, it can impact the prospect's decision to buy or the customer's decision to stay with you based on how well they are treated and how easy it was to conduct business with you.

A major goal when I was with WorkFront (which was a SaaS Work Management solution) was determining how Finance could help us simplify our processes from sales to service to ongoing support and renewals. For example, this included the process for negotiating a contract's terms and conditions, the process for invoicing and payment options, as well as the continued billing for services or additional products and services over time. We worked together with Finance to create the easiest ways possible for the customer to do business with us. Although challenging at times, we found many ways to keep the complexity behind the scenes and make the customer experience smoother so that it was easy for them to complete their business transactions while protecting the company with clear executable contracts.

The customer's lifecycle continually evolves. The customer starts with being intrigued by the marketing he encounters, then begins working with a sales representative, then with product experts, and, just before purchase, with finance team members to complete their purchase of the solution. And then they begin to implement the solution. In addition, they may require a services implementation approach using a proven methodology to ensure they receive the maximum value from the solution. This is usually executed by an educational and consulting team to help customers achieve the right level of knowledge and ownership to be successful. The services team goal is to create a baseline implementation that creates a solid starting point for the indispensable use of your solution at a minimum.

Customer success is maximized in these types of solutions by creating a formalized implementation approach that creates a detailed roadmap for the customer to follow. These methodologies would include following a traditional set of stages (i.e. Plan, Design, Build, Test, Deploy, etc.). This approach provides a set of tasks and deliverables at each stage to explain what is expected of the customer's team and what the customer can expect to be delivered by your implementation team. In essence, it becomes their plan for implementation and can be used to define a statement of work with a predefined scope of work.

One of my favorite customers during my Cognos days was a leader in athletic apparel. They were one of the first prospects for which we used our new Cognos implementation methodology to deploy our Finance solution. In reviewing the statement of work with the client's CFO, (which laid out each stage of our methodology with the list of tasks and deliverables by each stage of the methodology), his comment was, *"This is so simple to understand exactly what your teams are going to do for us and deliver to us for the price. I really don't have any changes. Most of the vendors we've worked with don't provide this much information."* In fact, clarity created one of the best customer experiences the CFO had experienced with any vendor.

This carried on into the implementation stages as well. At Cognos and Workfront, we invested in an internal education program to certify our consultants on our new methodology. This ensured that we had a consistent approach, which would produce quality and excellence in our delivery for every customer. The consulting team that worked through the implementation with each customer also provided feedback to the management team on a regular basis. As they were using this new methodology, the consultants stated that it made it easier for them to provide a clear roadmap of the plan to the customer and to deliver consistent progress reports. One of our successful consultants on this team told me that he loved how the communication plan in the methodology allowed for the services team to determine the customer's perception of how they were doing. It helped him to compare their perception to his own perception of how they thought they were doing. He commented that the implementation regular check in sessions revealed some miscommunications and misperceptions from the customer team that the consultants could correct quickly to keep the customer team moving forward. In this approach, the services team provided a positive experience for the customer team and the many end users who would be our future champions and evangelists.

Even during implementation, the customer will face issues with the product. When that happens, the customer is being introduced to your company's product team. So up to this point, the customer had worked with Marketing, Sales, Services, and Finance along their customer life cycle experience with you. Now, let's consider how the product team can positively influence a customer's experience.

When you think about the product team it may seem obvious that the customer expects the product team to make the product better and continue to innovate. However, we all know that no product is perfect, especially in the high tech industry. Bugs are the customer's number one area of concern. And they expect quick and complete bug fixes. I experimented with several approaches to improving customer communications in the face of product bugs to ensure that we understood the problem from the get go and then used technology more effectively to communicate progress and final resolutions.

At WorkFront, one of the most helpful tactics we implemented was the idea of a *way forward* solution. You might think of this as a work around solution to meet their needs without impacting the business until the bug fix could be generally released.

In the old days of all perpetual software, we would solve these types of problems with a "hot site" fix. It was technically a temporary solution to solve their one issue quickly. The product team then worked on the real solution that could be a part of the next main release. In some cases, the solution was actually tailored to solve a specific issue that was unique to them. However, in today's world of SaaS solutions, the notion of a "hot site" fix is not an operationally efficient way to solve customer problems even if they are unique to them.

So the WorkFront customer support team developed a methodology to find a way forward when customers discovered a bug that impacted their use of the solution. Sometimes this was a collaboration between our support team and the consultants to find a new configuration or design that would provide a similar result that was good enough to keep the customer moving forward with their day-to-day use of the solution. This gave the product team the time to develop the complete resolution and to release a higher quality product to the general customer base.

The product organization has a tough responsibility to the customer because they can't just stop working on the product release cycles in order to fix unique bugs. They have to work through a best practice methodology (i.e. Agile, Kanban, etc.) to provide the highest quality product in a timely manner. However, they are responsible for correcting bugs that do end up in the generally released versions of the software. From the customer's perspective they would like ALL of these fixed immediately. So how can the product team contribute to the customer's success?

One of our large customers that was a top marketing service firm was using WorkFront in a fairly complex manner. As I described earlier, I was meeting with them as part of my quarterly customer tours. After a lengthy discussion around the good news of how Workfront has been a valuable solution, we began going through their list of concerns. As expected, at the top of the list was their open issues of confirmed bugs. They needed to know when they were going to be fixed. My usual plan would have been to go through the list and try to determine which ones were production critical and basically getting a priority assigned to the list. However, I found myself asking questions about how they would like to see us provide information regarding their open issues. I asked: *"What would be most helpful for you to know to help you move forward with your use and expansion of the solution?"* The answer was surprising. They didn't say, *"Just fix them all."*, Instead, they made a simple request that we provide more insight into whether the problems would really be fixed and, if so, provide an estimated timeline, even if it was defined as late in the third quarter or next year. The issue was that the current status would always show "in progress" even if the product team never intended to fix it. They simply wanted transparency from us to be honest and state that it would not be fixed. In some cases, it was because the future product we were designing was going to do what they wanted in a very different way. The customer's response once I told them that was *"Great!, Just tell us that."*

What I learned from many other customers in similar situations was that they wanted enough information so their teams could make decisions on how they would continue their own progression and evolution of the use of the solution. It was very valuable to know where the product was headed from an innovation and roadmap perspective. This kind of information and feedback from our customers was vital to helping us make critical changes in our own backend processes to do a much better job of providing this information from our product team through our services team to the customer.

There was another concern that popped up during these customer tours related to our product information. The customers called it "The element of surprise." The customers loved the ability of a SaaS solution to provide continuous updates and innovations at a more rapid pace, however, sometimes the experience they had was one of "surprise".

They would log into our solution and begin to use it as they normally would. And suddenly everything was in a different place or didn't work as expected. This could be very frustrating, especially if they were under some deadlines and trying to get things done quickly. The request from the customers was for us to provide a "heads up" when any material changes were coming. This triggered some new processes and the use of our community website to provide more robust advance information. We also created a sandbox testing area for the customers to visit anytime and view the updated release using their database and review the changes that would be going live in the next few days. For larger customers, this was very helpful in their preparations, planning, and communications to their teams of any changes that they would be experiencing with the solution.

The moral of that story is that the customer's experience improved significantly because the services and product teams worked together on these solutions and processes to support improving the content, timing, and accessibility to the information in a more interactive manner. We focused on the customer's perception of our product quality and ability to provide good information in a timely manner. As a team, we then created a process to improve the customer's experience and maintain a solid relationship and partnership. This is a great example of how a well-planned customer life cycle can iterate on an on-going basis to continuously improve the customer's experience and their perception of you. It's the experience they have and the use of your product in an indispensable way that creates their perception of customer success. That is the customer success pot of gold that you are trying to understand and execute with quality and excellence in a consistent manner.

Once a customer is using your products or services as part of their day-to-day activities and operations, they begin to realize the value of your solution to improving their effectiveness. The next logical customer process is verifying they experience real value that will continue long term. But a major challenge after the solution is in production is to get key team members to adopt the solution on a broad basis so that measurable value is achieved. Most customers will perceive short-term value from a production solution, but it is usually within a small group or team. However, the team using the solution in production needs to get additional groups and teams using the solution in order to benefit from more robust capabilities, improved information or processes. Getting to a fully adopted solution is where the customer's ROI is.

Adoption of any solution has been the number one roadblock topic for a customer to getting the solution embedded into their operational effectiveness and realizing the value and ROI. In order to address this concern, I started asking more probing questions around this topic:

- What did they believe was the issue or roadblock for the teams to adopt?

- Did they observe a pattern, for example, a particular role or type of group?

- Did they ask the team members specifically what their challenges or difficulties were with using the solution?

Most of the customers had no answers other than their own impressions of what they thought were the issues. Researching further we learned that most end users didn't know how to use the new solution as part of their day to day job nor how it would improve their effectiveness. They saw the solution as just another application on their desktop and bothersome new system to learn. If they ignored it, perhaps it would go away.

While evolving the WorkFront implementation methodology, the issue of adoption came up early in my customer tours and was a hot topic at our user conferences as well. We conducted brainstorming sessions on how we can incorporate an approach within our deployment stage of our methodology to get enthusiastic user buy in on how the solution was going to make their job more effective and/or efficient. We needed to include a marketing message in our education program so that our clients fully understood *"What's in it for them."* We had to teach them how the solution would benefit them individually as well as creating value for their teams and for the company.

For example, our consultants would schedule one on one sessions with the various roles and teams to learn how they accomplish their basic tasks, processes or reporting in their current environment. We would then show them a better, quicker, more effective way to accomplish the same task, process or report using our solution. As we rolled this new approach out and asked for feedback on how well it was working, their overwhelming response was that it was the key to their successful roll out. The ROIs and value from the solution came to fruition much quicker as well.

These customers were also better positioned for their expanded use of the solution so we could begin planning the next phase of implementation. It was a very natural evolution for these customers and their experience, which contributed toward their loyalty. The customer feedback on my next customer tour with these customers, who benefited from our new approach, was one of a true partnership. The comments were *"Your team genuinely cared about helping us realize our success;" "Your team went above and beyond with every user to make sure they got it,"* and *"Your staff exuded passion and excitement which was contagious".*

At this point, you are beginning to see the trend behind making the customer's perception your reality in every aspect of your organization's approach to providing your target market with the best quality product and/or service. When you focus on meeting customers' needs in order to transform their ability to excel in their own markets, you create a relationship and partnership that endures long term. If you check in often with your customers to evaluate their perception of your company, product, and services, it enables your teams the opportunity to course correct and create an experience that nurtures and enhances your relationship and partnership. Do the right thing for the customer and everything else will fall into place. This customer-centric approach has contributed to the growth of the many software companies I have worked for over the years.

The following chapters offer a detailed and structured guide for you and your teams to utilize as a roadmap to follow to help transform your company into a customer-focused company. It is the approach your company takes in serving customers from the beginning of the customer life cycle through a continuous, easy to follow roadmap that creates an innovative partnership that ensures the ultimate success for your customers.

It will detail the Customer Experience Framework and models that I have used as a guide to helping each high tech company and my clients to create their own unique Customer Life Cycle model and approach by market to creating customer success.

Your teams will utilize this guide to help them define what success looks like for each of your market segments. That includes defining the right methodology for implementation and determining the outcomes and deliverables that create a customer for life. A Customer for life is one that has experienced high adoption and usage of your product along with a high indispensability factor. You will learn more about these topics in more detail as your work through the rest of the guide.

As you create your own Customer Life Cycle model, just keep playing the role of the customer at every point in the processes that touch your customers. By putting yourself in the shoes of your customer, you will see how they might perceive your company, its products, and its processes. You will understand how quickly and easily they understand what you do, what value you provide, and how you can solve their problem better than anyone else on the market.

Your own customized Customer Life Cycle will become your corporate way of life in developing and nurturing your customer relationship. It will be your organizational team's guide to how to serve and enable success with the various customers within each market. It will drive all your employees to see the customer's perception as your reality and find better ways to provide those customers with a transformational experience with your company and generate long-term loyalty.

CHAPTER TWO

The Customer Experience Model Framework

The CX Framework

A CX framework is a comprehensive model that not only incorporates the typical customer experience theories, but also provides a proven executable plan to deliver excellent results for both the company and their customers. The CX framework:

- Puts the customer at the very center of their operational plan.

- Takes into consideration all the touch points a customer engages with a company from inception to the ongoing long term relationship.

- Creates a companywide commitment to excellence in customer care.

- Makes it easy to do business with your company.

- Improves customer perception of your company compared to the competition.

- Differentiates you from your competitors in the market.

- Puts you in the thought leader position.

My experience executing this type of model for many of the top software companies today has taught me what works and what doesn't to optimize customer experience for various client types for each market segment. It makes customers understand that you really care about their success with your product and service.

One of the first companies who infused this type of model into their current approach to services was a financial reporting solution company, Hyperion. Their approach to services was to hire people with a financial background, teach them the software, and then send them out to the field to implement the solution once sales closed the deal. They offered a few courses they recommended a customer take and then it was up to the consultant to create the rest of the miracle. By changing the approach to a targeted model with a set of defined outcomes based on the type of customer and industry, we helped our customers find success with the solution using a best practice methodology. And we were able to increase the customer's ability to utilize the solution in a faster time frame showing an ROI in half the time from any of the competitors.

The framework for the CX model contains the following elements:

- A Customer Experience Maturity Model

- A Customer Experience Implementation Methodology that is used to develop, implement, and innovate the following elements:

  - A Customer Lifecycle Model

  - Customer Journey Maps

- Detailed Execution plan

- Measurement and strategic pivots

The following chapters will provide the details on how to build, execute, and innovate these elements to allow your company to execute a CX way of life for your company as part of your future.

CHAPTER THREE

The Customer Experience Maturity Model

A Customer Experience Maturity Model is a model that describes the levels of evolution that a company will go through in their ability to create a loyal customer for life in a predictable manner.

The first element of the Customer Experience Model framework is the development of a ***Customer Experience Maturity Model***. This model comprises the stages of a company's "maturity" in terms of increasing performance and capabilities:

- **Ad hoc**: Basic survival mode with exception-based activity and no plan

- **Aware:** Project focused with a baseline plan and priorities established

- **Repeatable**: Customer lifecycle-focused with repeatable quality and finally

- **Predictable:** Customer outcome focused with collaborative innovation capability; quick pivot strategy

Customer Experience Evolution – Figure 1

The model is important in helping a company define realistic expectations of their current capabilities to deliver an ultimate customer experience that can create a customer for life. It also helps produce honest assessments of the company's current capacity to deliver the end result: a mature customer experience.

The *Customer Experience Maturity Model* will help you design a roadmap for getting from your current less than ideal status to the **Predictable** status to deliver the ultimate customer experience. It will allow you to determine what's needed to develop the essential foundations to deliver on the new standards, processes, procedures, and deliverables. It will help you determine the level of reporting and monitoring required to measure progress. That will then enable you to pivot and make changes in an agile way. It will also show you the progression from survival mode to predictive mode. You will know when you achieve predictive mode because you will have control over your customer experience and be able to predict your quarterly outcomes within a range of 1% to 5%.

Each stage of the *Customer Experience Maturity Model* contains key attributes that describe the way in which you might be executing your customer's experience today.

When you are at a level 1 maturity (Ad Hoc):

- The priority is usually the latest crisis, what is front and center or requests that come from the loudest people or customers.

- Your team is not organized according to processes, roles or responsibilities that follow best practice standards.

- Your company has not created or communicated its vision.

- Metrics or numbers drive the strategy. The customer is not yet your focus.

- A soccer ball mentality is in place; everyone is chasing the same ball.

- In short, the company is operating in survival mode.

One of our client companies that offered a Corporate Performance Management solution exhibited the attributes of a Level 1 maturity level when I first joined them. After creating a basic framework with a simple methodology for their teams to follow, they were able to add more structure around the model that started to create consistent results in their customer implementations. This enabled them to move into a Level 2 maturity.

Customer Experience Maturity Model – Figure 2

Maturity	Ad Hoc	Aware	Repeatable	Predictable
People	Random, Skills/ Experience mismatched	Basic Organization structure Skills/Experience Defined	Process Centric Customer Experience Focus	Business and Customer outcome focused
Process	Ad Hoc Exceptions are the Rule Soccer Ball drives activity Everything is a priority	Identify Working & Nonworking elements Basic processes exist Integrated activities limited Priorities Defined	Customer Lifecycle established Repeatable Processes Metrics Established/ Monitored Feedback loop established	Customer Lifecycle Stages working collaboratively Integrated Customer Center Innovative Customer Success Program established
Technology	Basic Tools, Not right investments	Tools fit project or group, not integrated or collaborative	Tools/Systems Integrated with collaboration and social capabilities Automation	Real-Time, Collaborative Online Customer Knowledge/ Community Center
Business Strategy	Survival Mode	Project Focused	Standardized Customer Experience Delivery	Predictable Customer Experience Delivery
	Level 1	**Level 2**	**Level 3**	**Level 4**

When you are at a level 2 maturity (Aware):

- Priorities have evolved and are based on a basic vision and strategy to drive high-level metrics.

- Your team is organized with a structure to support the baseline strategy. Some standards and processes are in place to support the organizational operability.

- An Implementation methodology usually exists and drives the approach to customer engagements.

- A basic understanding exists of what works and doesn't. But this is not always documented or tracked.

- Metrics or numbers still drive the strategy. There is an increased awareness of customer importance. But strategy is not aligned to support a sound customer experience.

- Technologies begin to automate and track key processes, standards, and metric performance.

- At this level, a company is focused on project delivery.

The same company as described above continued to evolve the model after a few quarters. They began to track some key metrics around customer satisfaction, retention rates, expansion opportunities, quality of delivery, usage, and adoption. They began to structure the organization to align around key target markets and go to market strategies. The information feedback loop allowed them to begin iterating on their model and generate improvements in their key metrics and revenue targets.

When you are at a level 3 maturity (Repeatable):

- The priority is process and quality delivery-centric, with a focus around delivering the best customer experience.

- Your team is organized, with a structure in place that supports a customer life cycle and ensures metrics are delivered. Standards and processes support the customer life cycle delivery.

- You monitor and manage using technology to automate and interpret what's working and not working.

- Customer experience excellence and value drive the strategy.

- You analyze and pivot as needed on the strategy and initiatives to ensure continuous improvement in the customer life cycle model.

- At this level, the company is focused on best-practice customer experience delivery.

Within the same company after four quarters they were seeing consistent, repeatable results in their sales and services metrics and revenue goals. They were able to pivot faster in response to market changes and enter new target markets with a proven model for selling the right solution with the right services programs that created consistent results of value, quality and excellence.

When you are at a level 4 maturity (Predictable):

- The priority is based on innovating and evolving the customer's experience that creates a customer for life consistently.

- The organizational structure is collaborative. It supports a customer life cycle that ensures customer value and experience standards are met every time.

- Technology automates the monitoring and feedback loops to report and monitor results in real time.

- Customer feedback drives changes.

- The customer life cycle delivery drives the growth strategy.

- You analyze and pivot as needed on the strategy and initiatives to ensure continuous improvement in customer experience.

- You can predict the results and pivot quickly to ensure customer's value is realized.

- At this level, the company is focused on a predictable customer experience delivery.

With a proven approach in sales and services aligned with marketing and product, the same company was able to duplicate the model into other vertical market segments and grow the business exponentially using the same model and tailoring it for the solution and market with predictable results.

You will want to determine which level each organization has reached within your company. A customer experience model requires some level of collaboration and engagement from every organization in the company. This is an important concept to get across to your organizations for them to understand and support the journey they will be undertaking overtime as they go through the maturity levels.

Customer Maturity Model Risk Assessment

Understanding your end game goals is vital with a Customer Experience Model framework. Only when you understand how the maturity levels of your company's Customer Experience Model affect the customer's perception of your delivery and product value, will you have the guidelines you need to develop the best Customer Life Cycle model.

Customer Experience Risk Assessment – Figure 3

Indispensability

Understanding how your maturity levels effect the quality of your customer experience delivery and impact on the customer's use of your product

Two dynamics determine what type of customer your CX model framework will create; Engagement and Indispensability.

- Engagement represents the adoption rate the customer will realize at the end of the first round of your customer life cycle with your product. For example if the customer purchased 100 licenses and they have 100 active users fully engaged with using the product, they would have a 100% engagement rate.

- Indispensability represents the elements of the product being utilized that are critical to customer business needs and that make it indispensable to the company in their daily running of their operations or business. For example, when you have identified 3 key elements of your solution that are vital to your customer they will be very unlikely to replace your solution with a competitor's solution. These elements can be functionality, process and/or integration to other systems.

It is vital to understand each of these sections. Every customer will fall into one of these sections. You will need to assess in which of these sections your customer fits. Once you have determined your customer's risk level, you can tag them as being in that particular section in your CRM system and use it to help you assess the risky accounts in your customer base. Your goal is to move your entire customer base into the green section (*Loyal and Entrenched* in your solution).

When I begin working with many of my clients in the high tech industry they find that their customer base landscape consists of around 50% of their clients in the yellow, 30% in the green, and 20% in the red.

The following is a detailed explanation of the qualities that your customers will exhibit for each section.

The Red Section (aka Survival Mode) – This is the highest risk level. An example in this section is a customer that was sold 50 licenses for a few teams or groups to use; but only a few are using the software and in only a few areas of the functionality. It is not part of their daily, weekly or monthly work requirements for them to do their job or operate the company in any way. Your solution hasn't proven vital to their operations nor in improving their effectiveness in delivering their products or services. It is easily replaced with more than a 90% chance of non-renewal, no expansion or continued future use.

The Yellow sections (aka, Project focused or Repeatable) - This is the area of 50/50 risk. It means the customer can go either way with your solution. Some understand your value and some don't. But not enough of the majority or key influencers and decision makers believe in your solutions to improve the risk beyond 50%.

- A **Project Focused** customer: they will have purchased the solution to solve a particular problem, issue or concern. It could be one big project or it can be in one particular functional area that your product works well for them. They are a customer who has purchased a high number of licenses (i.e. hundreds or thousands of licenses) and are using it for only one thing. It has a high adoption rate, but a very low indispensability rate. There is not enough traction with your solution into the company's operations where they see it as a must have solution to operate their business more efficiently and effectively.

- A **Repeatable** customer: They will have purchased dozens of licenses for use in multiple teams, but only one team is exhaustively using the solution. They use many functions of the solution. It is more entrenched in their day to day activities and is used to improve their job capabilities or the company's operations, however, they cannot get the other teams or groups to adopt the solution in the same manner. The solution has a dedicated champion and a few loyal users who see the value, but the organization as a whole doesn't see the solution's overall value and ROI.

The Green Section – is the utopia section. This is where you want to position all of your customers. This customer was sold the right solution with the appropriate services programs and has the correct expectations for delivery from the very beginning. This customer has purchased 50 licenses and has all 50 licenses fully activated with at least 3 to 4 areas of the product and multiple teams in use. The teams find the solution indispensable to the company's daily, weekly and/or monthly activities for operating the business. It is essential to their ability to deliver their own products and services to their customers so that they can grow and scale.

Once your company has assessed the maturity levels for each organization and set a goal for the company, you are ready to develop the Customer Lifecycle Model. Your team would then develop a realistic plan for building your Customer Experience framework over time.

Each subsequent phase of your plan increases your company's performance and capabilities as you mature through the levels. In developing your plan, I recommend using an implementation methodology to ensure your team follows a best practice approach to developing and implementing the elements of the Customer Experience framework.

The next section explains this implementation methodology. You will build an iterative plan that moves you through each phase of maturity. You'll also be constructing the elements of the *Customer Experience* framework defined at the beginning of this section.

CHAPTER FOUR

Customer Experience Implementation Methodology

Build the Foundational Elements for the CX Model using a CX Implementation Methodology.

A ***Customer Experience*** methodology enables your company to implement or update a Customer Experience framework. It creates a standardized approach that ensures a high quality delivery capability of the team to design, develop, and test the elements created within the CX model to ensure quality and consume ability by the customer prior to implementing them in their daily, weekly, monthly, and quarterly operations or production, as illustrated below.

We will walk through each stage of the methodology in detail showing the elements the team will need to manage within each stage to create a quality customer experience approach.

The Customer Experience Methodology – Figure 4

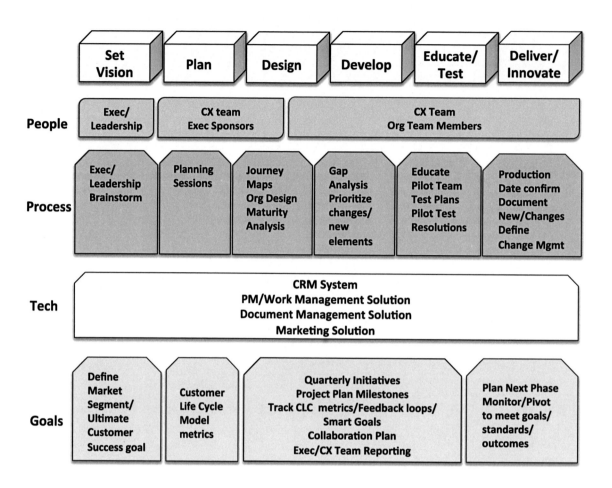

	Set Vision	Plan	Design	Develop	Educate/Test	Deliver/Innovate
People	Exec/Leadership	CX team Exec Sponsors	CX Team Org Team Members			
Process	Exec/Leadership Brainstorm	Planning Sessions	Journey Maps Org Design Maturity Analysis	Gap Analysis Prioritize changes/new elements	Educate Pilot Team Test Plans Pilot Test Resolutions	Production Date confirm Document New/Changes Define Change Mgmt
Tech	CRM System PM/Work Management Solution Document Management Solution Marketing Solution					
Goals	Define Market Segment/Ultimate Customer Success goal	Customer Life Cycle Model metrics	Quarterly Initiatives Project Plan Milestones Track CLC metrics/Feedback loops/ Smart Goals Collaboration Plan Exec/CX Team Reporting			Plan Next Phase Monitor/Pivot to meet goals/standards/outcomes

I. Set the Vision

The Customer Experience Methodology – Figure 5

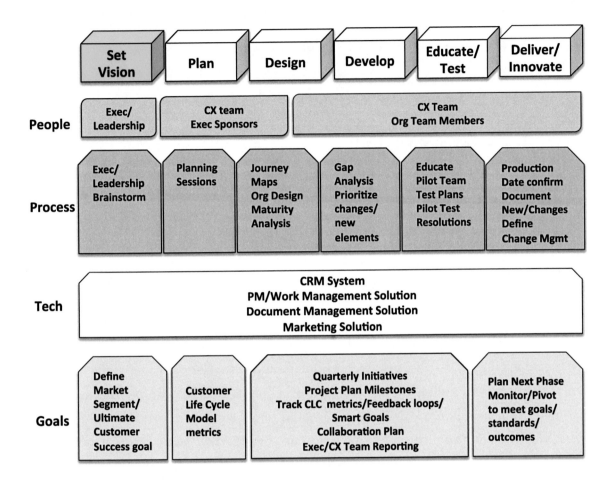

The Customer Experience Methodology diagram with phases: Set Vision, Plan, Design, Develop, Educate/Test, Deliver/Innovate.

People:
- Exec/Leadership
- CX team / Exec Sponsors
- CX Team / Org Team Members

Process:
- Exec/Leadership Brainstorm
- Planning Sessions
- Journey Maps / Org Design / Maturity Analysis
- Gap Analysis / Prioritize changes/ new elements
- Educate Pilot Team / Test Plans / Pilot Test Resolutions
- Production Date confirm / Document New/Changes / Define Change Mgmt

Tech:
- CRM System
- PM/Work Management Solution
- Document Management Solution
- Marketing Solution

Goals:
- Define Market Segment/ Ultimate Customer Success goal
- Customer Life Cycle Model metrics
- Quarterly Initiatives / Project Plan Milestones / Track CLC metrics/Feedback loops/ Smart Goals / Collaboration Plan / Exec/CX Team Reporting
- Plan Next Phase Monitor/Pivot to meet goals/ standards/ outcomes

Purpose: Developing a vision for the customer experience model, starts by constructing a baseline *Customer Life Cycle Model*.

Setting the vision

There are three elements that will need to be defined as part of your vision strategy and statement for your CX model:

    A. ***Customer Experience Corporate Climate Shift***

    B. ***A Customer Success Definition by Target Market Segment***

    X. ***A Customer Life Cycle Model***

A Shift in Corporate Climate

Building a **Customer Experience Framework** embodies all things oriented to servicing and delivering a high quality, consistent, and valuable customer experience to all of your customers. This is a COMPANY WAY OF LIFE. It is not a group or organization within your company that you create and assign them the responsibility for customer success   It is a commitment at the executive team level for all organizations in the company to do their part in contributing to ensuring the customer experience standards are always delivered from the first touch point through the on-going long term relationship. You must instill into all the teams the essential need to live and breathe a service-oriented approach and attitude. The company must truly believe that *the customer's perception is reality* and be committed to creating the perception that you are the best in the market.

Once you define your vision, you should market this internally to the entire company to begin the shift in the corporate climate so that each team member is committed to doing their part in delivering success for each customer.

In working with a smaller high tech company that delivers a project management solution, I had to spend some time with the executive team to convince them that a shift to this new mindset within the company was a key success factor to transforming their company to a customer focused company. They believed it was the job of the customer success team to create success for a customer. However, after reviewing their current performance metrics and seeing the decline in their results, they admitted they needed to address customer success differently.

They were losing customers almost as fast as they were selling them. They needed to correct their churn rates. I pointed out that it is ten times harder to bounce back from a customer's bad experience and turn it into a perception of success, when it has been sold and implemented in a disjointed manner. This company had three different and unaligned playbooks running in the company between sales, services, and product. Their customers were being told three different stories depending on what group they talked with. Therefore, the customer never understood the real story nor what implementation roadmap they should follow to find real value and success with the solution.

Defining Customer Success by Target Market

Build your approach to serving customers by defining your North Star. What is a North Star? It is the true definition of a Customer's Success. It is the definition you develop internally for each market segment that defines what success should look like for the customers in that market. It's not what you and your team believe you deliver to the customer—it's all about how your customer perceives how and what you deliver. It starts with the definition of value and/or ROI for the customer. Therefore, it's vital that you deliver to the customer exactly what they need to derive value from your solution so that you ensure high adoption and high indispensability (i.e. the green section defined on the CX Risk Assessment diagram shown on page 28), which we will discuss in greater detail in the next chapter.

For example, at Cognos, our go to market strategy included verticals by industry (i.e. retail, finance, manufacturing, etc.). For each of these industries, we would define a specific implementation roadmap with outcomes defined that ensured success for that vertical. The types of outcomes were designed to deliver the value in the form of the following:

- a set of reports for certain departments that were insightful reports that helped them to make decisions quicker to affect their end of quarter results.

- Knowledge transfer to the key members of the department to ensure they could create additional valuable reports and improve their analysis capabilities.

- Design the solution so the customer team members were using all the key functionality aspects of the product as part of their day-to-day activities, replacing what they were doing manually.

There are several ways to develop your standards for what creates Customer Success:

The Standard Approach ("The Rule"): The Rule is anything that meets customer needs 80% of the time. For example, the goal for every 8 out of 10 customers would be to ensure delivery of the following:

Meet the "Customer's Success Criteria."

Deliver product usage and engagement for 3 to 4 areas of the product's key functional areas that create the most customer value. We call this the Indispensability factor.

Receive customer feedback that rates you high in quality of service and product value.

Customer believes your product and/or service is embedded in their way of life and improves the effectiveness of their job execution or overall operability.

The Rule will form the basis for all your decisions for designing, developing, and executing your standard approach to your CX model.

The Exception Approach ("The Exceptions to the Rule"): This is the flexibility you create within your standard approach. In an 80/20 model, two out of ten customers will likely fall into this category. The processes you create to handle these exceptions are designed to change the customer's perception from bad to very good or excellent. The goal is to created approaches to handling these exceptions in way that still gets the customer to the success state you defined as indispensible and highly engaged. This will also ensure that you achieve your renewal and expansion opportunities and also preserve a long-term relationship with the customer.

Caution: Many companies get caught designing their customer success strategies and tactics around the Exception Approach. This leads to failure. I found it more successful to create your success definition around the Standard Approach (The Rule) and allow for flexibility in your approach to deal with any exceptions for those 'unique' customers.

Developing standards means starting out on the right foot from the beginning. ***What you deliver in your customer experience in the first 30 days will drive the long-term relationship.***

A customer's perception can go from great to terrible in one experience if the negative impact is large enough. When it goes bad, you will spend ten times more time, money, and resources correcting the customer's course from red to green and restoring trust.

Therefore, start from the beginning of the partnership to ensure that your customer always experiences something positive when engaging with your company at any level for any reason. It's best to build toward this vision, so that the exceptions you experience will be few and far between the rule.

You can even set a smart goal for your ***Phase I Customer Experience Model Implementation*** to have the results fall within the 80/20 rule. The goal would be to have eight out of ten customers experience the rule and only two experience an exception. As long as you define a great experience for dealing with exceptions, you can restore trust quickly.

This would be a more realistic goal to give your team some breathing room to experiment with various ways to create the ultimate customer success without fear of failure. It will take time and experience with your customers to get a real understanding of what success looks and feels like for your customers. In other words, what the customer perceives as valuable, game- changing or transformative within their organization.

You need flexibility in your plan to experiment with ways to:

- Deliver your product and services

- Understand what Customer Success is by market segment

- Manage your processes

- Monitor results

- Report, innovate, and implement changes smoothly

Your organization can then evolve in its maturity and experience to deliver the type of customer success that changes their perception of your company and the value of your product and services.

With these concepts in mind, you can create a good baseline definition of what customer success should be for each target market.

For example, one of my client companies that delivers a master data management solution, began with three different products; one for data analysis, one for data cleansing, and one for data transformation. They struggled with finding success in delivering a Master Data management solution because they would sell and deliver each of the products independently. They sold a vision around Master Data Management and all the values it provides, but couldn't deliver any of the value because of the segmented delivery approach.

Once the team understood the problem, they defined what created success in Master Data Management for each of the market segments (i.e. Retail, Manufacturing, and Financial Services). They then transformed their entire implementation approach by aligning the product roadmap and implementation approach to eliminate one off solutions and customizations. Their new implementation approach provided a clear, well-defined roadmap with defined outcomes and deliverables that were confirmed as valuable and game changing for their organization. This approach generated a significant increase in average sales price per deal, shorter sales cycles, and shorter implementation time frames within two quarters of making the changes.

The Customer Life Cycle

The next step in building a vision plan for your CX model is to build a Customer Life Cycle Model for your company. A Customer Life Cycle model creates a collaborative customer centric approach to engaging with customers. You are building a new way of life for how you operate and deliver value to your customers as a holistic company-wide team. It takes a CX village to raise a customer for life. This is your master plan for your CX village.

A Customer Life Cycle model usually contains at least four sections. They can contain up to six sections depending on what you define as the start and end points for your CX model. For example, you might consider when a customer engages with your company through a marketing tactic as the starting point and the ending point when they renew and/or expand. Most companies consider the starting point once a prospect is qualified as a potential opportunity.

In a Customer Life Cycle Model, you're defining the sequential stages of the customer's engagement with your company from the beginning point all the way to becoming a customer for life. The following illustration is an example of a Customer Life Cycle model for a high tech company. In this example, The Life Cycle model is broken up into four sections called "Acquire," "Implement," "Value," and "Expand." However, your team will define their own lifecycle sections based on the product and services your company offers. These sections may be different based on Business Unit Verticals or Segmentation (i.e.

Retail, Financial, Manufacturing, Healthcare, IT, Marketing, etc.) You should consider defining a different Customer Life Cycle Model for each business unit, vertical or defined market segment.

A separate Life Cycle Model is required when the product and target market are different enough that the definition of the approach, offerings, deliverables, processes, and teams need to be unique in order to deliver the success criteria that was defined in the first step above. If the definition of customer success is different enough for each market segment, then the team should design a Customer Life Cycle Model specifically to ensure the success definition is delivered consistently and repeatedly with quality and excellence.

CUSTOMER LIFE CYCLE Figure 6

A customers' first experience with your company usually begins with a marketing activity that draws the customer to your website. We'll begin the life cycle from the point where a prospect drops into a potential sales cycle. You can certainly start from the point where marketing is developing or nurturing potential prospects. You would simply add a section called "Business Development or Account Development or Demand Generation" and map your processes around the development of your leads to qualified leads.

Therefore, first consider the sales, or Acquire, section, which goes from qualified lead through a sales process to a signed contract. Other names to consider for these sections can be "sell," "land," "evaluation," etc.

The second, or Implement, life cycle section begins with the initial implementation to the actual use of your product or service in production. This section generally involves the introduction of a larger implementation strategy and methodology. Other names to consider for this section are "Launch", or "Deployment". Timelines are irrelevant here. We are just considering the major elements the customer experiences throughout the Customer Life Cycle with your company. This section usually follows an implementation methodology of some kind that is included as part of this section.

The third section, "Value", takes the customer from simply using the product or service through the embedding of the product into corporate standards. It then becomes a way of life for the company where the customer utilizes your product or service as an integral part of how they operate their company and how they provide quality products and services to their customers. Thus they realize the value of your solution. This is the section where you validate the company's achievement of the original "success criteria" (the goals the customer expects to meet with the purchase of your product) and "stickiness" (what makes your product indispensable). This is usually the area where a Customer Success program is activated as a way of providing additional support, education, coaching, and consulting as needed to ensure they can entrench the product or service within their organization.

This section ends when a customer is convinced that your product or service is providing essential value to the company or organization and they are ready to expand.

In the final section, "Expand," the customer has already realized value from the product and/or service. They then want to continue as a customer and to discuss expanding the use of your product or service throughout the organization or company. Obviously, once the company engages with an expansion opportunity to purchase more product or services, the sales cycle begins again and moves through the customer life cycle model once more. Thus you have made a customer for life, who goes around your sections smoothly and enjoys the partnership with your company.

Setting the goals

You need to set goals for each section of the *Customer Life Cycle Model*. These will become your main goals for managing the standards and outcomes expected from your CX model. These should all align with your company goals and objectives both short-term and long-term.

The teams executing each section of the *Customer Life Cycle Model* must clearly understand the goals. These goals are like bumper rails in bowling; they provide the team members with guardrails on how to measure, monitor, and adjust the processes, procedures or standards that will enable them to focus and execute successfully. When the team comes up with a new idea or a change to existing standards, they'll evaluate them against these goals and ask themselves: "Does this allow us to achieve the goal better or is it a distraction with different goals that are outside our current execution strategy?"

A significant challenge will be reining in and controlling all the ideas and changes that arise during the process. The best approach is to build a Customer Experience Committee from the original team, with representatives from all organizations in the company. This provides a control point for review and analysis. The team can also help determine impacts and implementation plans. The details of creating this team is discussed in the next chapter.

One of my clients with a project management and agile solution began executing on a new Customer Life Cycle model. They did a great job at creating many new elements required for a baseline implementation of their Customer Life Cycle. They didn't get the foundational elements across the functional organizations in place with feedback loops nor a rhythm for evaluating what was working and not working effectively. The team enjoyed some great short-term results. However, it quickly became apparent that the goals needed to be defined for each section, when the results were inconsistent.

- Why were some customers successful and others not?

- What was going wrong and where?

This is where the smart goals came into play and established the bumper rails needed to keep the team focused and understand when, where, and how things were going wrong. Once we put the goals in place for each section with technology to track these goals, they found it much easier to determine where the inconsistencies were and what was causing them. They were then able to make adjustments easily and quicker to get the results more consistently.

Remember that your goals are all about creating the best customer experience which impact the key metrics that drive results. Don't fall into the trap of designing standards, processes, and procedures that support your model by making it easier for the team members. This could end up delivering an inconsistent or poor customer experience. Too often members suggest changes that make their jobs easier or more lucrative, but don't improve the customer experience. The CX committee is the guardian of the process to ensure that your team takes a holistic view of the change.

Your goals should be challenging but achievable. Team members should be confident in their ability to deliver above and beyond their competition. Your customers should believe that you have delivered everything they need to succeed with your product or service. Remember "The Customer's Perception is your Reality". You always want to have an understanding from the customer's perspective when making changes to your business model.

Here are examples of general goals for each section of the life cycle model:

Acquire:

- Sales Cycle time

- Success criteria defined by market segment

- Customer satisfaction rating for sales experience = 4/5 stars

- Average Sales Price (ASP)

- Win Rate

Implement:

- Internal service level agreements (SLAs)

  - Kick-off/planning Session within five days of close

  - Clear transition/introduction from sales to services

  - Baseline use of product/service confirmed within 30 days of close

  - Customer implementation reporting is automated and visible to sales and services teams.

    - Customer satisfaction rating for consulting/education courses and support delivery = 4/5 stars or >=95%

    - All Success Criteria has been met

- Utilization rates (internal optimization of the team capacity)

- Time to Value (Time from contract execution to Go-Live)

Value:

- Product NPS score > 70%

- Customer usage/engagement > 85% for active users

- Adoption % = 100% (i.e., if purchased 100 licenses, all 100 licenses are activated)

- Indispensability Factor is > 4

Expand:

- Renewal rates > 90% (these can be defined by market segment)

- Expansion revenue = 40%

- Expansion Opportunity – within 6 or 9 months of Implementation start

- Predictability Metric (R/Y/G) (Risk Assessment metric)

- Total Customer Value $ average by Market Segment (Total Revenue $ potential of the customer)

Once you have created a well-defined vision for your CX model, your team can begin planning for the execution of the model. This will require a proper implementation methodology for the team to follow to ensure that the elements of the Customer Life Cycle Model have a solid plan. The team should agree on the implementation of their new approach to creating a consistent customer success with proven results.

The CX framework has a proven methodology that works well for implementation of a customer centric way of life for the company. The methodology has five stages:

1. Plan

2. Design

3. Develop

4. Educate/Test

5. Deliver/Innovate

CHAPTER FIVE

CX Implementation Methodology: The Plan Stage

Purpose: To define the plan and the team for the development and launching of the Customer Lifecycle framework by phase.

Building a Customer Experience Team

You need people on your team who believe in your vision for creating an end-to-end ultimate customer experience using your ***Customer Life Cycle Model*** as the guiding standard. Members of the team should represent each of the various functional areas of the company. A sample team would include members from the following groups:

- Sales

- Services (consulting, education, support, and customer success)

- Finance

- Product (a program manager, product marketing, QA)

- Marketing

- Distribution, if applicable.

The Customer Experience Methodology – Figure 7

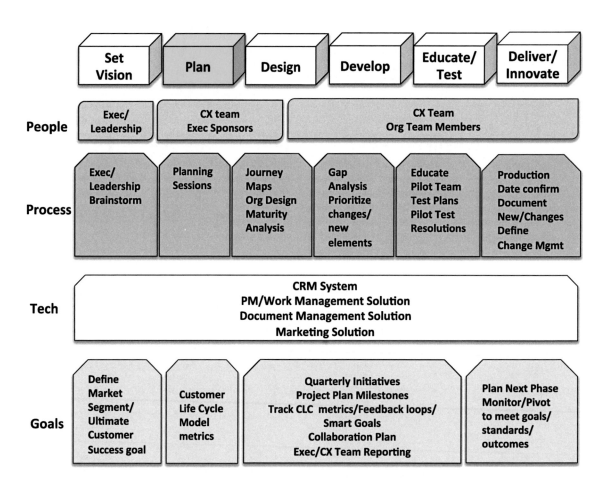

The team goal is to build an experience roadmap that clearly defines how and why a customer engages with the company.

It's critical that the Customer Life Cycle Model should include all the touch points a customer has with the company. In fact, many other employees interface with customers in addition to customer support, product, consulting, education, customer success, and sales. Remember, it takes a village to raise customers right and keep them long term.

The Executive Sponsors

Confirm that the Executive team members agree to be the sponsors. Their role is to lead the communication plan to the company to ensure that all employees understand the purpose of a customer life cycle and the importance to the company's strategy. The sponsors approve the required budget to develop, implement, and maintain the Customer Life Cycle as part of the company's way of life. This usually includes all the activities and head count required to implement and to maintain the model as the company matures.

As the CX Team evolves over time, it will present the overall plan annually for each phase, and the budget required, to the Executive Sponsors. As a pivot on the strategy is required from quarter to quarter, the team will present change requests based on the complexity, impacts, and costs of the change. Only those changes that exceed a certain budget or impact to the company should go to the Executive level for approval. The CX team should have members with authority to execute on more than 80% of the changes required in order for the team to fluidly iterate on the model.

Define the goals for Customer Life Cycle

The goals you define for the overall Customer Life Cycle should provide assurance that your customer is experiencing value and positive interactions with all company employees. These can be both high-level goals and also specific smart goals that measure various activities and programs.

Set up your goals by each section of the Customer Life Cycle. They are either an improvement to a current goal or a new goal defined to track a new program, activity or process and the outcomes from these. An improvement goal would be used when launching new programs or offerings or processes in which you expect an improvement in a current metric. A new goal would be a new metric that you are creating to provide insight into whether new elements or changes are working and making the impact on results that you expected.

Table 1. Examples of Improvement and New Goals:

Improvement targets:	New Goals:
Renewals improve by 5%	Customer Satisfaction rate > 95%
SLA targets improve by 10%	Traffic on self-help website increases by 25%/quarter
Number of Customer Service calls reduced by 15%	New Product/Service offering improves product usage by 20%
Expansion leads increase by 10%	Enterprise Account Engagement score for new accounts > 80%
Sales Win Rate improves by 20%	Services $/License $ % > 75%
NPS Score increase by 15%	Time to Value < 90 days

Each section of the Customer Life Cycle will have a set of Metrics. The team will identify the goals from quarter to quarter for each metric and measure the results.

For Example:

The Acquire section would be measured based on the following metrics:

- Win Rate

- Sales Cycle days

- Average Sales Price (ASP) or Average Contract Value (ACV)

- Services $/License $ (%) (Initial sale)

- Qualified Lead conversion rate (%)

The Implement section would be measured based on the following metrics:

- Time to Value

- Customer Satisfaction

- Adoption Rate

- Engagement Factor

- Utilization

The Value section would be measured based on the following metrics:

- Renewal Rate

- Usage Rate

- Adoption Rate

- Engagement %

- Indispensability Factor

- Customer Satisfaction or NPS score

- Average Customer Reference rating by segment

- Renewal Risk Factor

- Renewal Prediction %

The Expand section would be measured based on the following metrics:

- Customer Growth rate

- Revenue Growth rate

- Total Customer Value/Potential

The team would agree on the goals to set for each of these metrics. For those metrics that are new for the company, the team should track these for a quarter or two first and then set the appropriate target. For metrics that are currently being tracked, a new reasonable target should be set as the new target.

Define the Timeline and Key Milestones

The CX Leadership team should identify the summary level timeline for the Customer Life Cycle Model Implementation with key milestones.

The best approach is to implement the elements required to execute a baseline Customer Life Cycle for one market segment. Keeping the maturity model in mind, the iterations over time will evolve the Customer Life Cycle along the maturity model as well as the team's execution capabilities.

The Plan

The Customer Life Cycle model is an iterative execution plan. Therefore, the Customer Experience Team will always be planning the next phase of evolution as the company grows. The team will plan from quarter to quarter, modifying the plan as required in order to continue delivering on the company goals and objectives following the strategic plan.

I recommend using an online project management solution in order to plan collaboratively on the priorities and the required foundational elements needed to get to the next level of maturity. There are many options out there today, whether it be a (Software As A Service) SaaS or on premise solution. Based on your size and budget, I would do some research to find one that fits your needs with the capabilities required to manage your CX implementation and collaborative communication effectively. I personally like the SaaS solutions on the market today as they are cost effective with robust functionality and allow for worldwide collaboration if needed. At a minimum, the team should develop a summary-level plan with the priority elements identified by each Customer Life Cycle section that sets an implementation target date.

The Customer Experience Leadership Team should review the summary plan and give the OK for the team members to begin building out the details for designing, developing, testing, educating, and rolling out the current phase.

With a summary plan defined, the team can begin setting up weekly or biweekly meetings with the CX team and move into the Design stage of the implementation methodology.

When I joined WorkFront , it was one of the smallest companies that I had ever worked for. As I began to put my plan together to build the foundational aspects of a new implementation model, I worked with the Sales and Services team. I spent time sharing the plan with the team members and getting their buy in and feedback. The key transformational elements to get them involved in making the changes was explaining how they would benefit individually, as a team, and as a company.

By developing the plan in a formalized way, I could share the plan easily with the Executive team as well as the teams whose engagement and support I needed to execute in a timely manner. This was the first key step to successfully delivering the foundational elements within 90 days. Even the board was pleasantly surprised at the pace in which we were able to make the changes and impact the results.

CHAPTER SIX

CX Implementation Methodology - The Design Stage

Purpose: To design the detailed roadmap a customer will follow at each section of the Customer Life Cycle Model.

The Customer Life Cycle roadmap evolves from the Customer Journey maps that are created for each section of the Life Cycle.

Defining Customer Journey Maps for Each Section of the Life Cycle Model

A customer journey map is a roadmap to the executable plan for each section of the Customer Life Cycle. These are critical because they provide the details for developing the ultimate customer experience for every touch the customer has with your company. At each section of the Customer Life Cycle, a customer journey map will define the process, standards, people and/or services a customer will experience every step of the way during that section of the partnership with your company. There are two kinds of customer journey maps:

- A ***current*** customer journey map, which is what you do today

- A ***visionary*** customer journey map, which is what you want a customer to experience

The Customer Experience Methodology – Figure 8

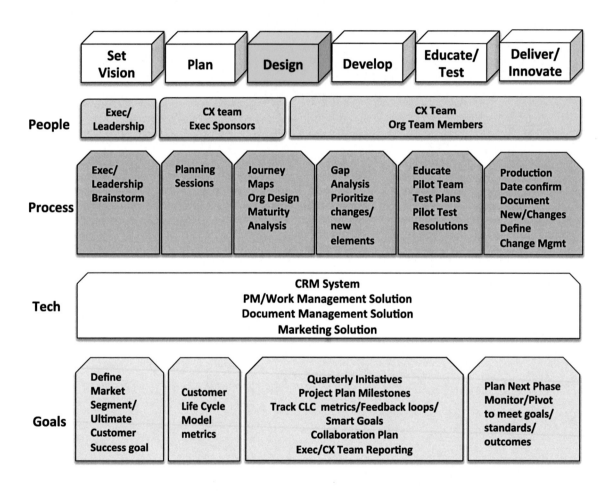

In this phase, the team will spend a few days or even weeks to brainstorm the right customer journey map for each section.

In order to develop the details behind each section of the Customer Life Cycle, you will need several design session meetings. In many cases, you can schedule one meeting for each section. The goal of these meetings will be to define the details of all the various processes the company currently has, or may be missing today, in order to deliver the highest quality and consistent experience with your products and services within that section of the Customer Life Cycle. As you develop the customer journey map for each section, review your vision, goals, objectives, and metrics and discuss the following:

Put yourself in the Customer's place and play the role following the process(es):

- Review what the customer sees, hears, interacts and perceives throughout the process in the section you are mapping.

- What's missing in order to deliver the highest quality of excellence in that process or deliverable in a consistent manner?

- What's not working today? How would we improve that? What would that look like?

- How can we measure the success of the new process in order to evaluate monthly what's working and not working?

- How can we automate certain aspects of the execution of the process as well as monitor our effectiveness within this section?

In consulting with another client that provides an Agile software solution, it was interesting to work through this exercise with the team. The team's tendency was to tell me what they did today and talk about the one off exceptions that they encountered. They had a tough time articulating what they should do to optimize the customer's experience. That's because they weren't really sure what the customer was experiencing. Although they had some verbal feedback on a few cases, they hadn't collected any data on the customer's perception of their company, their processes, and their product value on an 80/20 rule level.

If you find yourself struggling with this exercise, I encourage you to go on a customer tour of a variety of customers in the various market segments in order to uncover their real perception of the various processes they have experienced from sales to implementation to support and to on-going service. This will add vital data points to the development of the visionary journey map.

When I was at WorkFront, I went on a quarterly customer tour. Each quarter, I would visit at least 5 customers that represented each of our market segments. We would spend a few hours together going through an agenda that included hearing from them on what was working well and what wasn't working well, the value they were realizing from the product and services, what they would like to see from us in the future and then ending the meeting by sharing the product roadmap and new services, offerings or changes that were coming in the near future. The best part of the meeting was asking the customer how we could serve them better. This customer information was critical to the changes and pivots we made in the future to continue to drive improvements in the customer's perception of our company and products. It helped us uncover what was needed to get them to the indispensible state in using our solution which would enable further expansion opportunities.

Let's begin by going through an example of how to map out a customer journey, both current and visionary, for the Implement section, of the Customer Life Cycle Model.

You'll be defining your journey maps in sections, as defined here:

A. Map the current customer experience (in diagram format)

- Define the processes the customer goes through in each step along the flow for that section.

- Define the purpose of the process and benefit to customer.

- Identify key areas of customer concerns that impact success.

- Is there a metric that can be tracked for direct feedback on what's working or not for each process within each section?

B. Map a visionary customer experience (in diagram format)

- Define the processes the customer *should* go through in each step along the flow for that section.

- Define the purpose of the process and benefit to customer.

- Is there a metric that can be tracked for direct feedback on what's working and what's not for each process within each section?

- Make sure you resolve any areas of concern or issues that the customer faces today in doing business with you easily and with clarity.

- Develop processes you can deliver consistently with quality and excellence.

- The goal of this map is to create the processes, standards, work flows, and people to ensure consistent execution of the customer success standard you defined in the plan/design stages in order to create a fully engaged and entrenched customer for that market segment.

C. Identify any gaps between the two

Are there differences between the visionary customer journey map and the current customer journey map?

D. Define the people and their roles

Know who is required to execute each process, monitor execution quality, review exceptions, monitor customer feedback loops, and evaluate on a regular basis what's working and what's not. The roles should be defined with responsibilities and skill sets required to create quality and excellence for each process and section along the customer experience journey.

E. Set up customer feedback loops

Establish the feedback loops at various points in the process. Define teams to evaluate feedback data, make decisions on changes, and manage the implementation of changes. Remember the customer's perception is very important to understand the true state of your customer. Have you provided a real game-changing transformation to their organization with your solution?

F. Develop appropriate metrics and goals

These should be meaningful for the type of process, service and product being delivered that can be tracked as a smart goal. These can be made team goals and incorporated into a bonus plan to motivate the teams with the most impact on the results.

Let's discuss each of the above elements in more detail since this is where the teams will spend most of their time in executing the Customer Life Cycle Model. The Customer Journey maps will be your design for that section of the Customer Life Cycle model. Once you have theses elements defined, you will be able to put your detailed execution plan together and kick-off your Phase I of your Customer Life Cycle Implementation.

A. Map Current Customer Experience Journey Maps (in diagram format)

I recommend using a large whiteboard; a room with multiple whiteboards would be ideal. You can always take pictures and document into a Visio-type technology later.

The key to each creating a quality journey map is having the team brainstorm on each step a customer goes through, from the time your customer is introduced to your company or one of your product or services, through the purchase process, and all the way through delivery and ongoing support and service and finally the expansion of your solution.

The secret to the model is to develop smooth transitions from one section to another as they continue their long-term relationship with your company. There may be one particular transition that makes the most impact on the customer's perception of your company. This may be in the sales to service transition, in expanding the use of your products or in purchasing new products or services.

You will evaluate the entire customer process today. And then define each component of the process that your customer experiences today in detail.

B. Map Visionary Customer Experience Journey Maps (in diagram format)

Once you have a map of what you do today and all the processes the customer experiences for the implement section, you then can use another white board or wall to map the visionary journey map.

The best way to start is to imagine you're the customer. Keeping in mind the following goals:

α. Target market – What target market does this Customer Life Cycle represent?

β. Customer Success Definition – From the Vision that was defined earlier, you will have a clear definition of what a successful customer's implementation and/or roadmap goals and objectives are that create an Entrenched and Loyal customer (green quadrant of Risk Assessment diagram)

χ. Key metrics targets

For the Implement journey map, you would have the team start with the question of "We just closed a new contract, what is the next step for the customer?". This should be a transition process from sales to services to start the Implement section of the Customer Life Cycle. Once you define the first step of the process for the Implement section, the team should then define all processes along the Implementation methodology by each stage of your methodology. This would include desired outcomes and deliverables that are critical to getting the customer to the predefined success targets. You should consider anyone in the company that would interact with the customer during any of these details processes.

It's essential that your implementation team keeps the customer perspective in mind. Determine whether the processes and interactions enhance the customer's experience, improve their knowledge, make it clear as to what the next steps are for their team, and so on.

Start mapping out all the steps the customer experiences along the required steps or stages of your implementation methodology. Include meetings (onsite and calls), planning and design sessions with consulting, requirements understanding, building a "slice of life" system for unit testing and validation, test planning and execution, education programs for the customer team by role, support programs, the transition to customer success, etc.

Discuss the goals, objectives, and outcomes for each step. There are company goals you want to achieve at the end of the process; however, make sure you consider how best to accomplish those by delivering a customer experience that encourages the customer to want to interact with your company further. You want your company to be easy to do business with and one that cares about your customers' success.

For example, If you have a methodology with the typical stages of Plan, Design, Build, Test and Deploy; you define the processes and tasks for each stage of the methodology that the consultant would guide the customer through. You would include when and how the customer would go through an education program, interact with the product team and/or utilize their support program. You would also define the deliverables at each stage, the people involved, their responsibilities and authority levels. You would then define the goals and metrics the team will use to monitor the success of the execution of these processes and the customer's perception of how well you execute and delivered on the expectations you set for success and value. You would finish by defining the hand off processes between Sales and Services to start the implementation section and the transition from Services to Customer Success at the end of implementation.

If your business model targets multiple market segments, you'll need to consider the following:

- What do you do differently for each market segment (i.e., enterprise vs. corporate; retail vs. manufacturing; or marketing vs. financial)?

- Map each of these market segments separately defining the unique processes the customer would experience for that market segment.

  - *Note: Some elements of the process may be the same, but many may have to be different to ensure you meet the goals/metrics you laid out for that section around revenue $, % services $ to license $, time to value, customer satisfaction, etc.*

In these sessions of brainstorming with the CX Team, you'll find some very passionate discussions taking place. I would encourage you to let some of these emotions rise to the surface. They'll uncover some of the real customer issues and concerns your company faces. The key to these sessions is for everyone to be open-minded. The team must hear everyone's thoughts and suggestions. Much of the content from these sessions may not contribute to the final outcome, but the leaders within the team must listen for meaningful and actionable content.

Ask the following questions when you're exploring these ideas and challenges:

- Is this about making the employee's life easier or the customer's?

- Does it deliver a higher quality of product or service?

- Does it improve the customer's perception of our company?

- Does it make it easier to do business with you?

- Does it help the customer utilize the product or service in the best way possible?

- Does it create clarity for the customer about the company, products or services and how to get the highest value?

- Does it create an opportunity for the customer to consider an expansion or additional products or services?

- Do the outcomes and deliverables produce a transformational effect for the customer?

During these meetings, keep the vision statement the team created during the Vision stage visible to all in the meeting, either by writing it up on the whiteboard, putting up a poster or projecting a slide on a screen.. This is the definition of what a successful customer looks like for the market segment you are mapping out. Also outline the key metrics you're trying to improve in order to deliver results to the company that you defined for this section. Those metrics along with the vision for the customer's perception will help guide the team toward your North Star: The vision you expect to achieve when all is in place.

You will document five elements that make up a single journey map. These are required to define the support system behind the processes within each section:

- The process

- The people with authority and ownership

- Roles and responsibilities

- The metrics with targets or goals

- Policies and detailed procedures that need to be documented.

These journey maps have generated the most popular feedback from my customers. That's not just because they were a nice format for viewing the entire vision for a particular section. But, the journey maps also offer a clear and concise way for all the teams across the organizations to discuss:

- How they should communicate with their customers

- How they should service their customers with a clear vision

- How to work collaboratively on a common set of goals

- How to monitor and measure how they are doing using metrics

As the teams evolved, they update the journey maps to reflect the changes necessary to improve their internal processes and work flows including changes to responsibilities, metrics and goals. The clients also used these to present to their boards and other organizations. They became a method for the teams to discuss how they could help customers benefit more from their products and ultimately to become indispensable to their customers.

The next figure is an example of a customer experience journey map vision for the Implement section from the Customer Life Cycle Model sample, as shown on page 42:

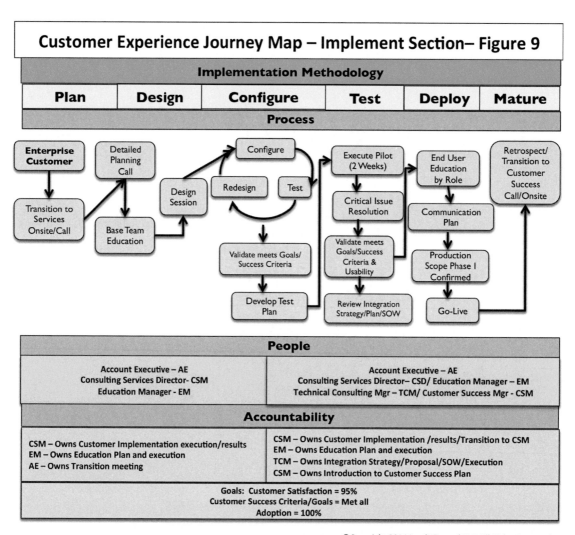

A map for the current customer journey map would be the same format as above. The idea is that the team would have this type of format on each whiteboard. One whiteboard would represent the current customer journey map; the other would represent the vision customer journey map. With the future and past presented, the team must analyze each map and document the gaps.

C. Identifying the gaps

The team will now document using a color-coded technique to identify the differences between the Visionary Customer Journey Map and the Current Customer Journey Map.

Using Figure 8, you can create an organized model that shows the gaps or areas of improvement based on color-coding. For example, you can create a color for each of the following within the process section:

- New processes (**Red**)

- Existing processes that work (**Green**)

- Existing processes that need improvement (**Gold**)

- Existing processes that need to be deleted (on the current map, you can put an X through the box)

- You can also color-code each section to separate the identification of the stage, the process, roles required, authority levels, metrics, etc.

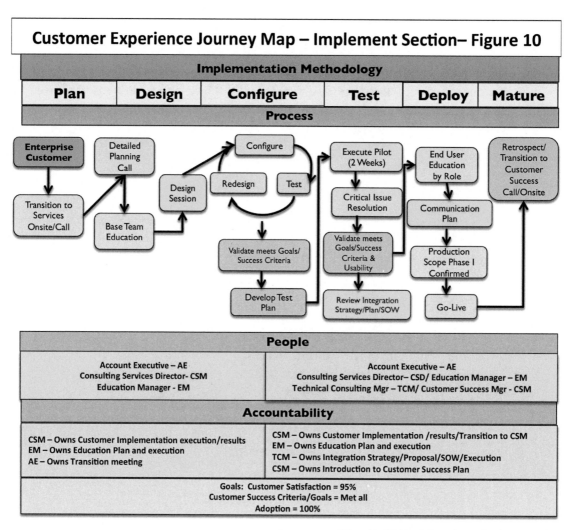

Customer Experience Journey Map – Implement Section– Figure 10

Implementation Methodology					
Plan	**Design**	**Configure**	**Test**	**Deploy**	**Mature**

Process

Enterprise Customer → Transition to Services Onsite/Call

Detailed Planning Call → Base Team Education

Design Session → Configure / Redesign / Test

Validate meets Goals/Success Criteria → Develop Test Plan

Execute Pilot (2 Weeks) → Critical Issue Resolution → Validate meets Goals/Success Criteria & Usability → Review Integration Strategy/Plan/SOW

End User Education by Role → Communication Plan → Production Scope Phase I Confirmed → Go-Live

Retrospect/ Transition to Customer Success Call/Onsite

People	
Account Executive – AE Consulting Services Director- CSM Education Manager - EM	Account Executive – AE Consulting Services Director– CSD/ Education Manager – EM Technical Consulting Mgr – TCM/ Customer Success Mgr - CSM

Accountability	
CSM – Owns Customer Implementation execution/results EM – Owns Education Plan and execution AE – Owns Transition meeting	CSM – Owns Customer Implementation /results/Transition to CSM EM – Owns Education Plan and execution TCM – Owns Integration Strategy/Proposal/SOW/Execution CSM – Owns Introduction to Customer Success Plan
Goals: Customer Satisfaction = 95% Customer Success Criteria/Goals = Met all Adoption = 100%	

Note: Gaps represent areas that need focus for changes to existing processes or developed as a new process or deliverable. These would need to be addressed as part of the execution plan.

The gap analysis will clearly illustrate the things that you must stop doing as well as what you must start doing.

D. Defining the people

Once you have the processes well defined you will define the roles required to execute each process. These roles will be responsible for taking ownership of the following elements for managing the processes assigned to them:

- Monitor execution quality.

- Review exceptions.

- Monitor customer feedback loops.

- Evaluate on a regular basis what's working and what's not.

The roles should be defined with responsibilities and skill sets required to create quality and excellence for each process within each customer life cycle section.

Using Figure 8, you will be able to define the various groups, roles, and responsibilities required at each step of the process to deliver the customer experience.

During the brainstorming sessions, the team may struggle with this concept at each step of the process for the visionary customer experience journey map. Many groups don't want to be responsible nor be measured, especially if they're not held accountable today to standards for delivery or customer experience metrics. Often the team cannot come to a consensus on the roles and responsibilities and who should own each particular element of the process and where the proper handoffs should be. In those cases, it would be appropriate for an Executive Sponsor to attend the next meeting and listen to the areas of concern. In many cases, it is wise to include the Executive Sponsors or Customer Experience Leadership Team members who represent the various areas , in order to obtain buy-in and agreement on the execution of these new processes and procedures. You'll need to have complete agreement on the following for each step of the process:

- Who owns the deliverables for this process and standards?

- Who owns the metric results?

- Who has authority to make the changes as needed in a timely manner?

You will notice in Figure 8 that there is a section to identify the roles involved at each area of the process and then below, a section that defines the authority and accountability level for each of those defined roles.

Customer Experience Journey Map – Implement Section– Figure 11

People	
Account Executive – AE Consulting Services Director- CSM Education Manager - EM	Account Executive – AE Consulting Services Director– CSD/ Education Manager – EM Technical Consulting Mgr – TCM/ Customer Success Mgr - CSM
Accountability	
CSM – Owns Customer Implementation execution/results EM – Owns Education Plan and execution AE – Owns Transition meeting	CSM – Owns Customer Implementation /results/Transition to CSM EM – Owns Education Plan and execution TCM – Owns Integration Strategy/Proposal/SOW/Execution CSM – Owns Introduction to Customer Success Plan
Goals: Customer Satisfaction = 95% Customer Success Criteria/Goals = Met all Adoption = 100%	

This is important to establish, because it will drive the proper execution and clarity for the team when implementing new processes and managing change in a production environment. It will become part of the corporate climate changes as the organization evolves in its maturity.

The CX team would develop a Customer Journey Map for each section of the Customer Life Cycle using the process defined in this chapter. There may be different team members required from each of the functional organizations for each of your Journey Map sessions. (i.e. For the Acquire section it would be driven by the sales team with the services and marketing leadership team members supporting, the Implement section would be driven by the services team with the sales, product and customer success team members supporting, etc.)

The end result will be a set of journey maps like the example in Figure 10 that represent each section of the Customer Life Cycle.

E. Setting Up customer feedback loops

The customer journey map should have a feedback loop from either the internal teams and/or from the customer at various points in the processes. The following are recommended for creating the most informative feedback loops:

- Define the points of feedback

- Define the type of feedback that is helpful to understand what is working and not working

- Define the teams to evaluate feedback data and make decisions on changes required

- Define the Operations team members to manage the implementation changes.

The hardest area of the model to implement and maintain is the evaluation of internal and customer feedback. Remember that the goal of a customer experience model is to drive continuous improvement in the customer's experience with your company, its products, and services in order to create loyalty. So if you simply implement all the changes and then sit back, you'll experience positive results in the beginning that taper off over time.

This methodology is designed as an iterative life cycle that continues as long as you are in business. This means that you must understand what enables you to achieve the goals for your Customer Life Cycle as well as what detracts from achieving those goals. In order to do this, you have to create metrics for measuring, monitoring, and evaluating the new processes, programs, offerings, and procedures you put in place as part of the new model. The monthly results will drive the decisions on pivot strategies or simple management decisions to keep driving towards excellence in your customer's experience.

For example, one of the metrics I put in place at WorkFront was a series of internal SLAs for monitoring the first 30 days of a customer's experience.

- The first metric measured the time from the close of the customer transaction to when the customer's planning session was conducted.

- The second metric measured from the customer's planning session to when the customer built a baseline application and the customer's team was actively using the solution or in a pilot phase.

- The third metric measured from customer's planning session to their confirmed Go-Live date.

These metrics were extremely helpful in understanding where our bottle necks were in moving customers through the implementation lifecycle as well as holding sales accountable for the proper hand offs, debriefs, and introductions to the customer team. They also measured time to value for our customers. We measured these by market segment so we could get a feel for the 80/20 rule on the standard expectations we should set for new customers on implementation timelines and commitment levels. The focus for these metrics was to ensure the first 30 days of the customer experience was at the highest levels of quality and excellence to set them up for success long term. We added customer feedback metrics at the close of the sale and at their Go-Live to get their perception of their experience with our team and our product.

Table 2. Example Metrics Companies Use Today:

Internal SLAs:	Customer Experience Goals:
Sales-to-service transition: welcome call within three days of contract close	Received a roadmap plan within ten days of close
Kick-off meeting within seven days of contract close	Initial Implementation Success Criteria has been met within 30 days of close
Initial implementation within 30 days of contract close	Education program met or exceeded expectations and provided solid baseline knowledge
Customer has had planning call to confirm plan within 7 business days of close	Ratings or review by course (4 out of 5 stars)
Customer is scheduled for initial education plan within 10 business days of close	Ratings or reviews of consulting team (5 Stars) Customer Engagement >90% Customer Indispensability >3
Customer Engagement Confirmation for consulting is sent and confirmed within 10 business days of close	Customer Support feedback is 4 or 5 Stars or 95% Customer Satisfaction rating or NPS Scores

These metrics can be collected automatically, using various technologies. There are two types of tracking you'll want to consider establishing:

- Internal tracking using a technology that allows the operations team of the organization to track internal SLAs. A project management or work management online collaborative system works best for tracking processes and customer implementations. It will allow you to calculate time in between dates to understand current performance on SLAs, as well as how long the processes are taking (i.e., average time to implementation production (a metric commonly referred to as Time to Value), SLA performance by process, etc.).

- Customer satisfaction ratings can be gathered for different processes as well. I suggest using various techniques for measuring the customer's perception along key processes. These can be simple ratings (i.e., four out of five stars), short surveys (no more than four questions) or simple Yes/No questions about meeting their expectations. If you're using customer surveys, ask short, specific questions about the particular part of the process and value.

The CX Leadership Team would review these metrics each week/month/quarter, depending on what is the right timing for each metric. The team would have the operations team collect the actual results for these metrics into a dashboard with the targets next to each metric and the variance to the target for review. A weekly/ monthly/quarterly rhythm of meetings should be set up to review these metrics and make decisions on pivot points to the strategy or changes required as necessary to move the results towards the targets.

The following are recommended meeting types for reviews:

- 15-minute online team meetings: Best for piloting new processes or newly implemented changes when the team needs fast feedback to make quick changes that impact monthly and quarterly results.

- 30-minute online team meetings: Best for processes already in place and for conducting a quick overall status and focus on solving top-priority problems.

- 1-hour meetings: Best for executive-level reviews with the team to discuss larger, more complex pivots to the strategy or major changes to the Customer Life Cycle model.

- 15-minute online team meetings: Best for piloting new processes or just implemented changes when the team needs fast feedback to make quick changes that impact monthly and quarterly results.

Keep the meetings to a minimum, with clear agendas that allow for maximum results. Using online technologies allows the teams to view required information to make decisions that maintain forward progress. The key to executing effective meetings is to be solution-oriented. Try not to get hung up on discussing the problems for too long. It is best to understand the problems and what is preventing the groups from delivering an optimal Customer Life Cycle and results; then spend the majority of the time solving the problem and determining the next steps and changes required.

Goals should be assigned to each metric. The team should develop reports that show if, when, and by how much the targets have been missed. If these are new standards, processes or procedures when you have no standard or history to review in order to create a goal, you may have to pick an initial target that allows the team some breathing room for the first quarter or two. Then figure out later what a reasonable standard should be. Remember, you don't want the team to lose their excitement or motivation by putting an unrealistic goal on these metrics. It will just make the team give up in the face of impossible goals. However, you should make the goals challenging. If the team still pushes back on the goal and believes it is set too high as a target, explain that it's a stretch goal and is meant to extend your capabilities to establish a more mature organization that delivers better results for customers. Small steps should still produce results by establishing changes that improve the company's ability to deliver a better customer experience.

Developing customer ratings, adoption, and engagement metrics

Ensure that these are meaningful for the type of service and product delivered that can be tracked as a smart goal. These can become team goals for each quarter and be incorporated into a bonus plan to motivate the teams with the most impact on the results.

The metrics defined for an overall customer rating and adoption metric can be more complicated. There are several aspects to each of these metrics.

Customer ratings have the following elements:

- Customer's perception of the value the solution has brought to the company

- Customer's experience with how easy it was to get to a desirable usage of your product or service

- Customer's experience with how easy it is to do business with the company

- Customer's perception of the people they worked with during their customer experiences

- Customer's perception of the quality of service and knowledge of the people they worked with during their experiences with the product or service they engaged

Customer adoption and engagement metrics include the following elements:

- How many licenses or products or services did they purchase?

- Of those purchased, how many have been used or are actively used today?

- How often are they using the solution?

- Are they using the features and functions for the intended purpose?

- Are they using the elements of the solution that result in the entrenched use of the solution as a vital part of operating within their organization or company?

- Is their usage of the solution growing over time?

- Is their usage of the solution a vital part of doing their day-to-day operations?

- Does the use of the solution make them more effective, more efficient, reduce costs or grow revenues?

- How does your solution make their job, operations or ability to deliver their solution easier, better or more efficient?

Note: This is getting at how indispensable the product is to the organization

One of the most transformational developments we made in the Customer Life Cycle measurements at WorkFront was the development of a predictive model using our customer data on adoption, renewal history, and product usage. We plugged the data points collected around our customer's activities and usage of the product into a statistical model and found some interesting predictors of renewals and expansion activities. Armed with this information, we were able to utilize our limited resources more productively in order to provide a higher level of service to the customers that needed it. We were able to divide and conquer thus hitting all of our goals each quarter while growing our accounts with limited headcount.

The Customer rating information is usually collected by a services team member or operations team (e.g., customer support, education, consultant or customer success representative). Most companies use a 1–4 metric system to evaluate the answer to each of the questions. The reason for the 4-metric (and not 5) is to force the customer to decide if their perception or experience was good or bad. In a 4-metric system you may use the following type of definitions:

4 – Excellent, above expectations

3 – Good, met expectations

2 – Fair, did not meet all expectations

1 – Bad, did not meet any expectations

If the customer has a number that sits in the middle, it's likely that he will go for the neutral decision, which isn't possible in this 4-metric evaluation. He either had a good experience, a 3 or 4, or a bad experience, a 1 or 2. What I like about this approach is that it allows for teams who are in the beginning stages of their maturity model to allow for a good result to be a 3 (good). A 3 in most cases meets the 80/20 rule as well, meaning that 80% of your customers who experience a 3 will remain customers. Again, the goal is to set reasonable goals for the team to achieve so they feel successful for all the hard work they put into making the right changes. Obviously, if the results are still a 1 or 2, then the team will acknowledge the need for more changes or a pivot on the strategy.

Obtaining good customer feedback information was a key pivot point in optimizing the Customer experience at WorkFront. The Services teams (Consulting, Education, Support, and Customer Success) all had different feedback mechanisms in place that helped the teams to make quicker decisions on changes to our approaches, timeliness, and quality of deliverables throughout the customer's engagement with our teams. However, when we first starting asking customers about their experience and perception, the answers weren't very positive. Remember my mantra *"The Customer's Perception is our Reality"*. We focused on the areas where we had the majority of the feedback on the same topics and elements of our services and engaged with the customers to develop changes to our products and services to change their perception.

The good news was that the corrections were all relatively easy to make. As a focused team, we made the changes quickly. In fact, the results of the surveys turned positive by the within a few quarters. Within three quarters we had all service (education, consulting, and support) areas above the 95% customer satisfaction ratings in all the key areas we measured and 100% of our customer interviews had a positive perception of our company and product. The residual effect was the increase in customer expansion opportunities.

Developing a maturity level analysis

Once you've defined your Customer Life Cycle Model with the detailed Journey Maps for each section of your Customer Life Cycle, it's time to assess where each unit or organization is located on the maturity model. Most teams can review a maturity model like the one presented earlier in Figure 1 (and repeated here as Figure 11) and determine intuitively which level their organization is at on the maturity levels.

However, a true assessment reviews every aspect of the customer life cycle and determines the maturity level at each section for all organizations that must contribute to the execution of each element of the life cycle.

For example, in evaluating the design of the Customer Life Cycle, several organizations must touch the customer in service or delivery. Each organization must be evaluated to determine its level of maturity. You may find that the Product organization has already put standards, measurements, and customer service feedback loops and metrics in place and could be at a level 3. At the same time, the Services organization could be at a level 2 and Marketing organization could be at a level 1.

Customer Experience Maturity Model – Figure 2

Maturity	Ad Hoc	Aware	Repeatable	Predictable
People	Random, Skills/ Experience mismatched	Basic Organization structure Skills/Experience Defined	Process Centric Customer Experience Focus	Business and Customer outcome focused
Process	Ad Hoc Exceptions are the Rule Soccer Ball drives activity Everything is a priority	Identify Working & Nonworking elements Basic processes exist Integrated activities limited Priorities Defined	Customer Lifecycle established Repeatable Processes Metrics Established/ Monitored Feedback loop established	Customer Lifecycle Stages working collaboratively Integrated Customer Center Innovative Customer Success Program established
Technology	Basic Tools, Not right investments	Tools fit project or group, not integrated or collaborative	Tools/Systems Integrated with collaboration and social capabilities Automation	Real-Time, Collaborative Online Customer Knowledge/ Community Center
Business Strategy	Survival Mode	Project Focused	Standardized Customer Experience Delivery	Predictable Customer Experience Delivery
	Level 1	**Level 2**	**Level 3**	**Level 4**

Much depends on the company's internal organizations. If these organizations all report up through different executives or leaders, they may all work with different management styles. Some are more sophisticated and experienced than others. The first step is to understand how each organization views the company landscape. Then the team can understand the political obstacles that they will need to overcome in order to get all the organizations functioning at the same maturity level.

The essential reason to understand the maturity level of each organization is to determine the goal for the first phase of implementing the Customer Life Cycle company-wide. The following is an example of simple evaluation of the functional areas of the organization:

For example, if the Sales organization overall is at a level 2 and the Product organization is at a level 3 and the Marketing and Services organizations are at a level 1, then the first phase goal should be to get all organizations executing at a minimum level 2 in order to create a consistent Customer Life Cycle. From there, the company can improve performance through the maturity stages and optimize the customer experience appropriately within each section of the Customer Life Cycle and as a team. By achieving these goals, the company will avoid having one organization creating an amazing customer experience in a few areas of the Customer Life Cycle, while another organization is still trying to get the foundation in place to create some kind of consistency to their ability to deliver quality and excellence in a timely manner. This is what creates a roller coaster ride in the customer's experience along the Customer Life Cycle. This uneven company performance creates an inconsistent customer experience and risks losing customers.

The Action Plan

Here you will define the details of the plan with task definitions and assignments to the team.

The most successful implementations give authority along with responsibility. Make sure the assignments you make are not only a good match of skills and experience with the ability to execute, but that they provide the authority to make key decisions.

The use of a technology is essential for the team to provide an automated approach to real-time updates, collaboration, ask questions, get information, and share status updates. Such tools are a critical requirement for enabling efficient and effective management of the standards, processes, and procedures you put in place and track the results for all the metrics that get established. It can create automation capabilities and provide more capacity within the team to spend their time in higher value tasks and management duties.

Document the plan so that all Team Members can review and agree to the plan. It should include timeline and assignments and then be presented to Executive Sponsors to review and approve.

Make sure the goals and objectives for the stage being planned are clear to the Executive Sponsors, as well as the Customer Experience Team.

The key to successfully managing to the plan is to adopt the following policy:

"No excuses, only solutions."

The Executive Sponsors and key leadership team members will want to coach the team to follow this policy for everything related to customer experience. The core concept is that if you are assigned an activity, you have the authority and autonomy to do whatever is required to complete that activity with quality and excellence, on time, and within budget. In order to accomplish this, Team Members must always be thinking of solutions to every problem or roadblock that presents itself along the way. If they can't see a way to resolve the problem or roadblock, they get help from the team, the Executive Sponsors or leadership team to either resolve or clear a roadblock.

You don't want team members showing up to a weekly or daily status meeting with nothing but excuses. You want the team members discussing what got done, the possible issues they are facing, and what they're doing or going to do to get it done. Time is the enemy. It ticks away quickly when you allow team members to use issues and roadblocks as excuses. You want the team members to raise the flag the minute they're facing problems in order to get the right people involved to achieve a resolution. If they still have roadblocks, they should contact the Customer Experience Leadership Team or Executive Sponsors to get support and clearance to continue making progress toward their deliverables.

If the entire team conducts themselves this way, the implementation plan will succeed. And all future phases and iterations will go smoothly. Their behavior will become part of the corporate climate and maturity of the organization to implement new elements and to make changes with diligence and perseverance.

Setting the Timeline

Once you've built the team, have your Executive Sponsors and Customer Experience team in place, have determined the goals, and planned for the first phase of the Customer Life Cycle implementation, you will determine a timeline. The timeline should work from a realistic start date so that Customer Experience Team Members can book time into their weekly calendars to focus on the delivery of their project assignments. Then develop your timeline based on tasks and resources assigned, taking holidays and PTO into consideration. Add some slack time for critical path elements. Make sure you include tasks that can work in parallel to consolidate the timeline.

If you end up with an end date that is unsatisfactory to the Executive Sponsors or the Customer Experience Leadership Team, then review the plan in detail with the Customer Experience Team Members in order to validate that the time assigned to each task is accurate. Questions to ask:

- Are there any opportunities to decrease the allocated times on each task?

- Did you miss any opportunities to have tasks work in parallel to other tasks?

- Is there too much slack time built in?

- Can you utilize other resources to help deliver more activities in parallel?

- Are there opportunities for you to outsource tasks to get more done quicker?

Once they have fine-tuned the plan with the most accurate information and a delivery date, then the Team Members will need to schedule a meeting with the Leadership Team and Executive Sponsors. The team should present the best business case for extending the end date for final delivery and get their approval.

The best way to get team buy in is to evangelize the plan to the CX team and all additional team members within each of the organizations that will contribute to the execution of the plan. The milestone dates are important for the team to understand and agree to for a collaborative team to work together effectively to deliver.

Have a Communication Plan

If it's important to you, then be certain to make the value of the CX Implementation project vital to everyone who will be affected by the final delivery.

Create a marketing plan for communicating the following about the project:

- What will this deliver to the business?

- Why is this important to the business?

- How will it change the way we do business?

- What is the value to customers?

- How will it impact the department or groups within the organizations that it effects?

- What's in it for the employees affected?

- How will it affect these employees?

- How can they help this project be successful?

- What is the timeline?

- What is expected of them as part of the project delivery?

By educating the organizations affected and sharing with them the details of the value of the project, they will be able to internalize the information and begin to support the team in any efforts required. Evangelizing in a fun way is always encouraged, especially if you can find ways to make fun of yourselves and the way you may do things today. Then show the new and improved customer experience. The team could have fun creating a video of typical customer experiences today, with as many fun scenarios as possible that everyone would relate to—and then showing what it will look like in the brave new world and the tremendous impact on the customer's success.

Now that the company supports the work of the CX Team, you should also define a communication plan for the team during the implementation phase. That plan should be part of the new company corporate climate going forward.

This usually includes a daily wrap-up session, a brief 15-minute online chat or call that allows everyone to participate in a quick round robin discussion of critical items. The team members will either report "all is good" or share an issue that needs leadership support or resolution. This daily session can be a place where a team member is encouraged to ask for advice if needed.

The team should have a formal 30-minute status meeting once a week or biweekly, with a set agenda that includes the following elements:

- Introduction of new or changed Team Members

- Summary status of the overall progress of the Customer Life Cycle implementation

- Executive-level communications, which may include an announcement on strategy changes or new strategies that might need to be considered in the current execution plan.

- Round robin by major functional area (sales/services/marketing/product/finance/etc.)

    - What's completed with any highlights they might want to advertise

    - Issues that need the team's support

    - Upcoming changes in the organization that are important for the team to be aware of.

    - Review of Smart Goals' performance to date (once the initial phase of your customer Life Cycle is underway)

Monthly or quarterly, the team should present to the Executive Sponsors the overall progress of the Customer Life Cycle model delivery. The agenda is a condensed version of the above, which highlights key successes, deliverables, and positive influences on Executive level key metrics.

As logical as it may sound to have a good communication plan, you would be surprised at how few of my client companies had a formalized plan. A lack of formal communication from the Executive team down to the team members and back up the chain can prevent progress of the key initiatives determined by the Executive team for the quarter. An executive team can easily decide on a few key initiatives that turn into projects; they can then assign them to someone to manage and even have some of them be implemented successfully. Where most companies struggle is in maintaining a focus on ensuring that these key initiatives and concepts that require a companywide focus and engagement continue to innovate and evolve over time without losing the vision behind them. Successful communication plans ensure that these initiatives continue to progress and innovate.

Now that you have a solid CX Plan and Design that the team has agreed to and communicated out to the company, the CX team is ready to begin developing the new elements and changes identified in the design stage.

CHAPTER SEVEN

CX Implementation Methodology - Develop Stage

The Develop Stage:

The purpose of the Develop Stage is to develop the detailed elements that each organization must execute and deliver to support the execution of all sections of the Customer Life Cycle.

At this point, the CX Team should have designed and documented a journey map for each section of the Customer Life Cycle: Acquire, Implement, Value, and Expand.

For each of these journey maps, the team will have completed a gap analysis that defines the difference between what the company does today and what they want to do in the visionary journey map designed for the section. This gap analysis will create a list of requirements that must be developed or evolved from an existing standard, process or procedure to support the delivery and outcomes defined in the journey map. The Team will allocate these tasks to each of the appropriate organizations.

The Customer Experience Methodology – Figure 13

The following is an example of a gap analysis from the journey maps (today vs. visionary). This will become your roadmap for developing a more detailed project plan for executing the delivery of the elements in a phased approach that will lead to the new visionary Customer Life Cycle:

Figure 14

2015 Plan Customer Life Cycle Implementation Summary Action Plan (Gap Analysis)		
	Q1	**Q2**
Acquire	Incorporate Scoping Session into Sales Methodology standards for Market Segment	Create Transition Process from Sales to Services
	Create Marketing Materials for Internal/External messaging around Customer Life Cycle	Develop new SOWs and SKUs for New Services Programs
	Create New Program offerings with Product and Services Program	Create Value Selling Workshop for Sales team
	Create Education/Marketing Workshop to communicate Customer Life Cycle Model to Company	Execute Workshops on new Customer Life Cycle Model
	Create New Program offerings with Product and Services Program	Pilot Selling new Solution Programs
Implement	Define Customer Success that deliver Prescriptive Outcomes with values (programatize offerings)	Develop Customer Life Cycle Model Metrics Dashboard
	Develop New Services Methodology	Create New Maturity Model for Market Segment
	Develop New Templates for All Supporting Document Deliverables for each stage of the New Methodology	Create a Education Program to deliver knowledge transfer to meet Customer Success definition
	Develop Services profitability model	Create Baseline Implementation Definition
Value	Create Process for Consultant to transition account to Customer Success	Determine system for tracking CS program by customer & action items
	Create Customer Success program by Market Segment	Define Customer Dashboard and key metrics
	Create a model for CS team to utilize key services resources for solving customer problems	Educate CS team on new programs and offerings to support expansion opportunities
	Create processes for CS to incorporate required resources to resolve customer issues (using Cons/Edu/Support/Product teams) as needed	Create process for transition Customers from CS to AE for processing expansion opportunities back through the Sales Cycle methodology
Expand	Create process for AE to be supported by CS and Services to support Expansion opportunity closure	Create Process for Partnering CS/AE to ensure renewals and expansions are cohesive and easy for customer to get what is required done easily

The gap analysis lays out quarter by quarter the top-priority items that must be developed or changed in each life cycle section. The team can develop a gap analysis by putting all of the gap items on sticky notes and affixing them on the whiteboard under each stage name in order of what is most important. There are some items that must be done before other items can be done; in these cases, they are usually addressed in one calendar quarter and the next item is addressed in the subsequent quarter. If there are items that can be accomplished quickly, you can do them in the same quarter back to back. Once you have all of your gap items identified for each stage in a priority order, the team will assess the approximate time for completion and assign them to the right calendar quarters and team member. For example, if you are currently in Q4, then you would start your plan to begin the development cycle for these items in Q1. From this layout of all gap items by section by quarter, you can update your project plan with the details of implementing the requirements for the Customer Life Cycle.

The project plan will detail all tasks for changes and development requirements identified in the gap analysis. I recommend that you define the Customer Life Cycle section and all the tasks required to implement the elements of the journey map for this section of the life cycle. This means that the gap analysis might have identified 20-plus elements that you need to address. However, if the Phase I CX Implementation plan is to improve from a maturity Level 1 to a 2, you'll only put on the development list those items that support these stages of maturity progression. You'll add the rest of the items in the follow-on phases of your Customer Experience implementation plan. They could all be done in Phase II or might have to be split into a Phase II and a Phase III. Remember, one phase of a Customer Experience implementation plan could be 60 to 90 days. So with a focused team supported by Executive Sponsors, you can take your company from a customer experience maturity Level 1 to a 3 within a year. This helps you plan all the changes required to get to each of your visionary journey maps over time with a phased approach.

In the Develop phase, the team should have a plan for the detailed list of elements being changed or developed as new elements for the quarter. Each quarter the team should have assignments for delivering these elements within or by the end of the quarter.

The Plan may be updated at the end of the Develop stage based on a better understanding of what it will take to build, develop, test and roll out all the elements defined in the Gap Analysis.

If an element requires a true test period or formal pilot, then the team will develop all the content, processes, procedures, etc. in the current quarter and have it ready to pilot in the next quarter. This would include making sure the team allows enough time to educate the pilot team prior to the start of the pilot testing. If the element only requires a short period of time to develop and put in place for use in daily operations and execution, then no formal testing or pilot may be needed. In this case, the element can go straight to educate, document, communicate, and then launch.

CHAPTER EIGHT

CX Implementation Methodology - Educate/Test Stage

The Educate and Test Stage

The purpose of the Educate and Test stage is to test the new changes and elements to ensure they work properly and they deliver the expected level of customer experience. This is the correct stage to make changes and ensure they will create the impact that is expected. Once they are ready to roll out for the day-to-day delivery or operations of the business, then you will need to educate the appropriate team members internally. Some elements will only require an internal education program. But some will also require notification and education for the customer prior to rolling to production use or day-to-day operations.

At this point, you will have developed the required elements, made changes to existing elements, and created some new processes, standards, procedures, offerings or content that you are ready to implement. However, you must test these new elements and changes in order to verify they will deliver the type of customer experience that you have designed.

Therefore, you need to plan for testing the new offerings, content, processes, procedures, and policies that you have developed. Once they have been tested in a small pilot with a few team members and a select few customers for feedback, you can then determine the appropriate date for making the changes effective or for launching new elements. Then you need to plan an education program for rolling out internally and for announcing and notifying customers, if it's appropriate.

The Customer Experience Methodology – Figure 15

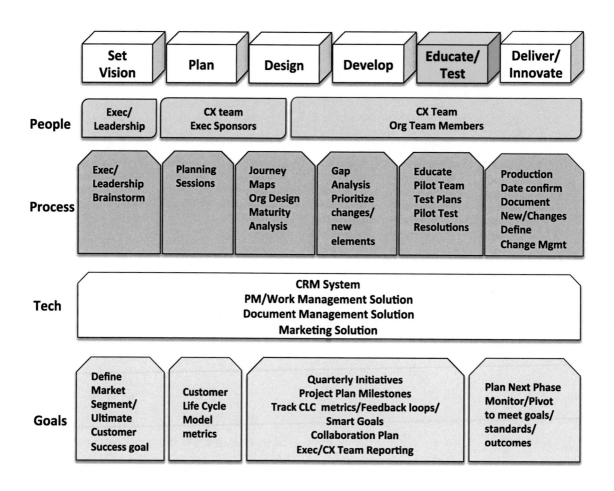

The Test Plan

Several levels of testing are recommended for each element, whether it is a new offering, content, policy, process or procedure,—or a slight change to one of these elements.

A Simple Test Plan: For a simple change or new element being implemented, you would create a test plan that documents the process in the appropriate reference guide. These guides can include playbooks, operational reference guides, etc. Determine the date the new or changed process will take effect. Have a few Team Members review the details and provide feedback to ensure that it will deliver the expected results and experience to the customer/prospect.

A Complex Test Plan: For a more complex change or new element being implemented, you would also create a test plan that documents the element in the appropriate reference guide. These guides can include playbooks, operational reference guides, etc. Determine the date that the new or changed process will take effect. In addition, you should create a test team to test the element in a pilot program from two weeks to 90 days, depending on the element. For processes, procedures or policy changes, a few weeks of testing with live prospects or customers usually suffices. For new products or offerings, I recommend a 60- to 90-day testing period.

Let's use the example of a new product offering developed on the Acquisition journey map to meet the requirements of a Mid-market segment. The test plan would be as follows:

- Use the new marketing document that defines the new product offering, what's included, implementation plan, and price.

- Use the new pricing policy and prospect qualification requirements.

- Identify the Mid-market sales team members who will pilot selling the new offering in the next quarter.

- Educate the pilot sales team on the new process, qualifications, and policies around the new offering and provide the reference documentation. Usually this would be put into their CRM (e.g., Salesforce, etc.) library of documents.

- Identify services team members required to support the process.

- Determine a pilot start date. If the current quarter is Q4, the pilot would start in Q1.

- Create a feedback loop process using technology to automate documented issues/feedback during the pilot.

- At the 30-day mark, evaluate feedback and make any changes for the second half of the pilot.

- At the 60-day mark, complete the pilot and evaluate all feedback and customer perceptions of sales cycle and value. This will require the development of a questionnaire being sent to the customers that purchased the new offering and asking for feedback using a short, four-question survey.

- Make all final changes (process, standards, outcomes, pricing, sales and marketing materials, etc.) to create a production ready offering.

Test/Pilot Results Evaluation

The pilot team will be required to provide feedback within a set period of time that is based on the pilot cycle time. For example, if the plan includes a two-week pilot, then the results feedback should be evaluated at the end of each week. If changes are required, then a retest may be required in order to ensure the results meet expectations for the new element or change.

All feedback from the pilot team members should be evaluated by the appropriate organizational leaders or members of the CX team to determine if a change is required. The goal is to improve the customer experience and to drive the company results in the right direction. If the change becomes a distraction or is not appropriate, the leadership team needs the authority whether to decide to keep it as is or to determine the change required to get to the expected results.

This is the point in the implementation process to make changes and to retest them. That ensures that the changes or new elements meet the requirements and expected results for improving the customer experience within the life cycle section.

Once the test results have been accepted, the team is ready to develop the education plan to ready the teams for the roll out.

The Education Plan

In the education plan, the team leaders will need to formulate a process for educating the team members who will be responsible not only for implementation and executing the elements or changes, but also those who will be required to support the changes. These are team members identified in the peripheral area of the Customer Life Cycle model. For example, in the Customer Life Cycle figure shown again here from Figure 4 in an earlier chapter, the outer square arrow figure defines the groups that support that Customer Life Cycle section.

If we look at the Implement section, the supporting roles are Education, Product, Customer Success, Support, and Marketing. You may need to include many of these team members in the education plan to ensure quality and consistent execution of the changes.

The CX team will need to evaluate how many sections are affected by the change and who is involved in the execution points along the Customer Life Cycle for the change or new program being implemented. The team would review the roles required to support the change or who would be effected by the change and include them in the education plan.

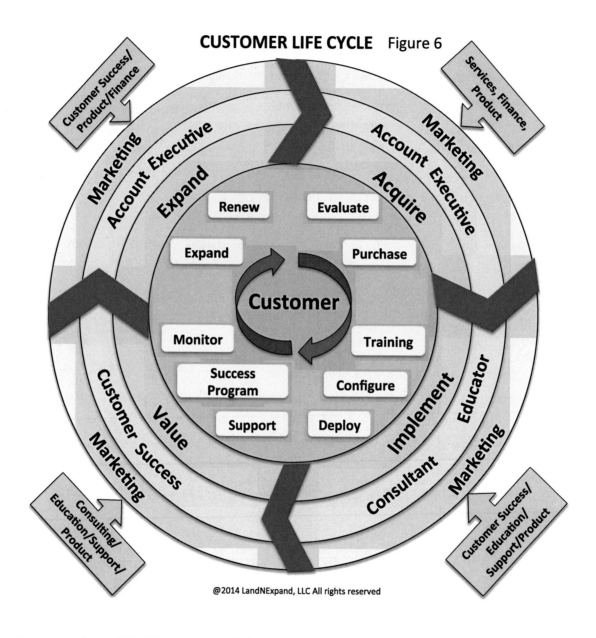

CUSTOMER LIFE CYCLE Figure 6

For example, at WorkFront, we rolled out two new service programs, one to support the Enterprise Market segment and the other to support the Mid-Market segment. Because these were new programs that utilized a new sales approach, implementation methodology and customer success program, we created an education workshop that we rolled out to all organizations and to which we invited all the leaders. We videotaped the sessions and allowed the leadership teams to educate their teams utilizing these videotapes as a way to get all team members informed and ready to support the new changes. The workshop included changes to messaging, value propositions, marketing materials, processes, policies and procedures as well as ways to get everyone in the company aligned.

We then created a pilot program, where one focused sales team in each market sold and executed the new program with the services team for one quarter. We monitored feedback both internally and externally (from the customer). We then made changes necessary to ensure the programs were more consumable and clear in the outcomes and expectations. We made some internal changes as well in our processes and procedures to make the experience smoother and positive for the customers in each market. We then rolled out the program companywide for all teams in both markets in the following quarter.

There are various ways to educate your internal and external teams to prepare them for the changes and new elements. Each type of element may require any one of the following kinds of education approaches.

Table 3. Education Approaches

Education Approach	Description
Notification	An online collaborative notification system in which a select distribution group can be created and notified of a new or changed process, procedure, policy or offering. This can also be a simple email
Update or New Reference Guide	These can be playbooks, policy and procedure documents or operational guides. They can be stored on shared/collaborative technologies and notifications can be sent to authorized document users.
eLearning	An online education solution that has a library of various education videos, Word and/or PowerPoint decks that are self-paced learning reference materials. They can be used for internal or external educational programs.
Workshop/Classroom Training	Instructor-led in-person educational course offerings with materials to support the training of any new or changed process, procedure, policy, or offering. Workshops are usually short training sessions of one to three hours. They can be conducted using online technologies to present the training materials and allow for interactive discussions and questions. Classroom training is more formal and usually involves one or more days of training to educate the team on various topics. In both cases, they can be video-recorded and put up on the library to allow for self-paced training. This works well for global rollouts to accommodate different time zones
Testing	Some educational sessions are best served by having a test or case study with a presentation as a validation that the employees have consumed and understood the critically important materials. Testing holds the team accountable for learning the required material in a specific timeframe

Once you've determined the development elements that require testing and education, you can plan for the right type of testing that ensures all team members have the proper education and understanding of how to do their jobs.

The education plan should be scheduled within a few weeks from launching a pilot test phase or from launching a change into production and day-to-day activities. The following is an example of an education plan:

Education Plan – Figure 16

Role	Courses	Timeframe	Venue
Sales Team	Sales Methodology Workshop Selling a Roadmap to Success Services Offerings	Q1	Virtual/Onsite
Services Team (Education/ Consulting/ Support)	Selling a Roadmap to Success Services Offerings	Q1	Virtual/Onsite
Customer Success	Sales Methodology Workshop Selling a Roadmap to Success Services Offerings	Q1	Onsite/ELearning
Finance	Services Offerings	Q1	Virtual/ELearning
Product	Services Offerings	Q1	Onsite

Many of my clients have utilized their internal education teams to support creating the content and conducting the courses or workshops for each educational requirement. If you do not have an internal education team established yet, you will want to engage one or more of the team members that has experience in creating educational content, conducting education courses and workshops. You can also utilize the marketing teams to help create videos and presentation materials.

Notice that these workshops and trainings are scheduled by quarter, based on when the project plan is scheduled to rollout the new programs and changes. Some workshops and trainings will continue each quarter to support new and transferred employees, promotions or job changes as part of their onboarding program. For example the sales certification and services certification programs should be quarterly offerings at a minimum. We recommend trying to organize new hires and internal changes into classes and then scheduling these certification courses so that you can have people work together in teams and support each other during their onboarding certification program.

After the testing and education programs have been scheduled and executed, the team will need to plan for the production rollout of the new product, services, offerings, policies, standard, processes, and procedures in support of the Customer Life Cycle implementation.

CHAPTER NINE

CX Implementation Methodology - Deliver/Innovate Stage

The purpose of the deliver stage is to roll out new elements and changes into the day-to-day operations for the appropriate teams responsible for executing.

This is the point at which the team is planning for the rollout on the scheduled effective date. Now the team can create a readiness plan for executing the new element or change as part of their daily operations.

Once the effective date is confirmed by the team, they need to execute the following production readiness activities within one to two weeks from the effective production date:

The Customer Experience Methodology – Figure 17

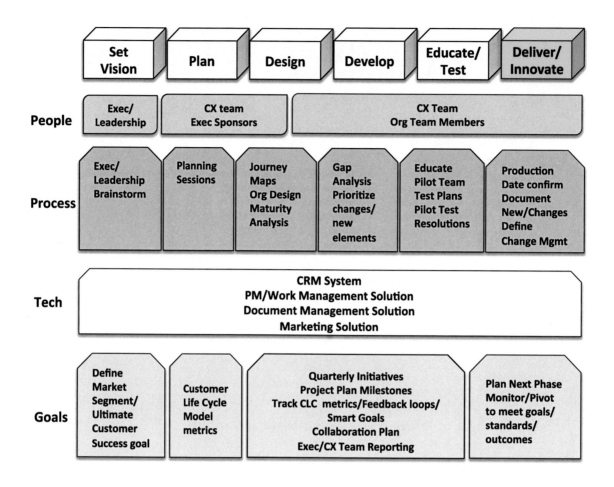

Documentation: All new or changed product, services, templates, documents, contracts, offerings, policies, standards, processes, and procedures have been documented and delivered to the collaborative technology being used to house and share gold copy versions of these documents for the teams to reference.

Review and Approval: The Customer Experience Team should determine if a review of the documentation to ensure accuracy and an approval from the appropriate leadership team members is required. If so, the document should go to the appropriate team member for review and approval prior to sending the final gold copy to the appropriate library.

Change Management process is formalized and documented. A notification has been sent across the company to ensure all employees are notified of the change and so that they understand how to submit change requests and provide feedback on any areas that are not working well.

Communication Plan: Develop a communication plan and cadence for evaluating what's working and not working in each of the customer life cycle sections and in the new changes that have been rolled out. Schedule monthly business review meetings with the Customer Experience Team and key Leadership Team members to evaluate the metrics dashboard and performance of key smart goals and results. Schedule weekly business reviews within each organizational leadership team and team members.

Next Phase Plan: Develop the plan for the next phase of the evolution of the Customer Life Cycle model by creating the plan for the next set of priorities for implementation.

Let's discuss each of the three Production readiness activities in more detail.

Documentation

There are many perspectives on documentation. Too often most documentation is either not utilized as intended or ever read again once it is created. However, our perspective is that most documentation is not user-friendly. It is not created in a short, concise, easily organized, and easy-to-find way so that the team members can utilize the information most effectively. We won't discuss best documentation practices here, but we suggest the following key guides to use in support of a typical rollout:

Sales and services playbook. This document would contain these key topics:

- Products

- Services

- Sales, implementation or service approach methodologies

- Pricing and packaged offerings

- Standards and policies

- Discounts and approvals

- Procedures

- Certification requirements

- Partner program

- References

Services Methodology. This document would contain these key topics:

- Methodology Diagram

- Statement of Work (Methodology defined within the SOW)

- Deliverable Templates for each stage of the methodology

- Customer Confirmation Process

- Customer Roadmap by market segment and solution

Customer Experience Guide. This document would contain these key topics:

- Customer Life Cycle Model

- Journey maps for each section

- Key metrics to measure success with current goals

- Customer success program

Operational Excellence Guide. This document would focus on how to make it easy to do business with your company and ensure the customer's experience with any organization will be met with quality and excellence. The following are key sections in this document:

- HR Section with all the key topics for employees (employee orientation, equipment, support, PTO, policies, procedures such as time tracking, expense reporting, etc., training, etc.)

- Onboarding process including certifications required.

- Finance section with the key topics for how other organizations interact and collaborate with the Finance team (e.g., sales support, services support, budgeting process, expense reimbursement, customer inquiries, standards, policies, and procedures, etc.)

- IT section with the key topics for how the IT organization supports the rest of the organizations (e.g., equipment, software, service, support, locations, help desk, policies, processes, and procedures to get the support required)

- Marketing section with key topics on how to request marketing support for events and collateral in support of each of the organization's offerings, mostly sales and services, but can be utilized for internal company activities as well. (i.e., processes, policies, and procedures would be included in this section.)

- Product section with key topics around standards and processes for new product releases and updates to existing releases including references to websites and information for the customer to find easy answers.

- Sales section with key topics for getting the sales team involved to help support a customer and summary information on partner programs and how a company can become a partner.

- Services section with key topics on how to implement and support a customer with the methodology, standards, policies, and procedures for how customers can engage and what standards the company holds themselves accountable to (i.e., customer support service-level agreement goals, product warranties, uptime standards, etc.) The services section generally includes consulting, education, support, and customer success organizations.

These documents should have various team members assigned to the appropriate sections and held accountable for the accuracy and updates to the information. If a change is required, they should submit the change through the leadership team and Customer Experience Teams prior to publishing any update.

If you are using a CRM (e.g., Salesforce, etc.) system with a library, the gold version of these documents can be published in the CRM library or a shared document storage technology that the team members can easily access, no matter where they are located. It's best if these documents can be indexed with search engines that make it easy to find the topics a team member is looking for. Reminders and notifications can be publicized to the entire company when a new version of any of these documents is published and given a reference to the section that has been changed.

Review and Approval

Each document should go through a process of review and approval by members of the Customer Experience Team and the team members responsible for execution of the area of change to ensure accuracy and alignment with the company goals.

Each document will have different team members assigned to each of its sections. These team members will be accountable for updating the sections as changes are processed through the change management process. They will then submit these to the appropriate functional leadership and Customer Experience Leadership Team members for review and approval prior to publishing.

Any of the organization's operational or administrative staff can do the administrative work on creating, updating, and publishing these documents using the technology of choice.

Change Management

This is the most common area that falls apart in day-to-day execution. Most companies do a good job of creating new programs, policies, procedures, etc. Yet they fail when it comes to managing changes to each of these. Why is change management so important? If you don't create and follow even a basic change management process, you will lose the quality and excellence in the Customer Life Cycle model execution and not benefit from the results long term.

A change request can be a simple form published online within your intranet to which all team members have access. I would recommend that each organization create its own internal change management process with its internal leadership team. The forms can be standardized across the company to simplify the process of submitting all requests to the appropriate Leadership Team. If the change will impact other organizations or have a significant change to the customer's experience, then it may also require the approval of the Customer Experience Leadership team. Once the organization's leadership team approves the change, they can submit to the Customer Experience Team for review and approval. The organization will then be responsible for executing the change using the best practice processes described in the methodology section of this book for rolling out changes.

The following is an example of a change management form used to request a change to an element within the Customer Life Cycle model:

Figure 18

Company Name					
Customer Experience Model Name					
Change Management Request					

Customer Lifecycle Stage	Implementation				
Type of Change (Check the box)	Product	Service	Process	Policy	Procedure	Standard
Describe the Change Request					
Areas Impacted					
Estimated Costs **Estimated Implementation Time**					
Metrics Improved					

The Communication Plan

In developing quality and excellence in the CX model delivery, one of the key success factors is a solid, well-executed communication plan. Such an effective communication plan supports the discussions of day-to-day activities, issues that arise, and the development and delivery of quick resolutions.

This plan shows a top down and bottoms up communication plan, as illustrated in the next figure:

The layers of the communication plan ensure the messaging flows both upward and downward in an effective manner.

- Executive communication

- Leadership communication

- Team members' communication

- Communication rhythm

Executive communication: *Key elements around the strategy.*

It is vital for each organization's Executive to communicate a consistent message around the year's top initiatives, goals, and objectives to the leadership team. They should share the top concerns and issues about results, indicating what's working and what's not working. This enables the leadership team to maintain their high level view of the company when they are working with their teams in order to execute the details of the strategy. It also allows them to keep the teams focused on planning, executing, and monitoring their own initiatives, projects, and changes that align with delivering to the top line strategy.

Leadership communication: Pass down the same consistent message on the strategy, goals, and objectives both to their team members as well as sharing the Executives top concerns based on the results. They will discuss with the team how to modify or improve their current execution plan to help correct the areas that are not working well or that are not producing the planned end results. It is also an opportunity to discuss if a strategy is worth pursuing and if some of their current plans should be scrapped and a new plan put in place that would drive to the results better.

Team Member communication: The opportunity for the team members to voice their view of how things are really working at the ground floor. They are usually on the front lines and executing the details of the plan. They see and hear from the customers and other internal team members what is causing some of the issues. This critical information enables an understanding of the real areas that need to be addressed and what should change. Often an entire plan doesn't need to be scrapped. Instead team members will create some modifications to the current plan that will pivot just enough to provide the customer the value and experience that produces the desired results. Moreover, they can also tell you if the customers are responding at all to the new offerings, services, product changes, etc.

Team members are a great source of real information about how to provide better value and experiences to the customers based on the daily feedback they get from customer conversations. These team members will provide the best insight into how a customer perceives their experience with your products and services. Customer surveys will tell you part of the story, but the front line team members will tell you the rest of the story.

By providing an opportunity for team members to participate in the discussions of the strategic plan and what they think needs to be modified or added you can create a powerful buy-in that creates a sense of accountability and desire to see the changes succeed. Getting the teams behind the leaders is a powerful component to achieve success quickly and to sustain it over the long-term.

Communication Rhythm: *The schedule of various types of meetings or communication vehicles.*

There are several types of effective meetings. They are usually short, concise, and effective in making decisions quickly.

- Daily Stand ups

- Weekly Top Priorities

- Monthly Results Reviews

- Quarterly Business Strategy Reviews

This may sound seem like a lot of meetings. However, keep in mind, that the goal is to monitor the business actively in order to make decisions quickly, which, in turn, drive results more rapidly. If the team doesn't communicate regularly via a mechanism to engage in discussions, to receive answers, and to get approvals to act, then pivots will happen too slowly and growth will lag rather than accelerate.

Here is a typical Communication Plan that would be setup for an organization.

Table 4. Sample communication plan

Meeting Type	When	People
Daily Stand Up	Mon – Fri at 10 a.m.	Team Members/Leader
Weekly Top Priorities	Mon 9 a.m.	Leadership Team/Executive
Weekly Top Priorities	Tues 9 a.m.	Team Leads/Leadership (Dir/Mgr)
Monthly Results Review	First Wed after Month close 2p.m.	Leadership Team/Executive
Monthly All Hands	Second Monday after Month Close 9 a.m. (replaces daily standups and weekly top priority mtgs)	All Team Members/Leadership/Executive
Quarterly Business Strategy Review	Second Tues after quarter close 9 a.m.	Leadership Team/Executive

These communications sessions would be scheduled on everyone's calendar as established meetings in this regular rhythm. There will always be exceptions that you can adjust for as required. However, the best policy is to make these meetings mandatory unless a team member has their leader's approval not to attend or to dial into the meeting. You may have to adjust times for worldwide situations to accommodate for various time zones.

The agenda for each of these meetings can be customized to be the most effective to enable and equip the teams to be successful in their daily execution. The main topics are usually the following:

Daily Stand Ups

- Top Issues

- Major areas not working

- Concerns/Questions/Clarifications

- Success Story

Weekly Top Priorities

- Top 3 priority Issues/Concerns

- Major areas not working

- Top Customer strategies that need to be addressed (High dollar)

- Change Management discussions

Monthly Results Reviews

- Review Organizations Dashboard

- Review Actuals to Budget and Forecast

- New or changes for Budget Considerations

- Organization Headcount Plan

- Progress of top organizational Initiatives

- Change Management discussions

Quarterly Business Strategy Review

- Review Company Dashboard

- Review Actuals to Budget and Forecast

- New or changes for Budget Considerations

- Organization Headcount Plan

- Progress of top company Initiatives

- Is Strategy Working? Why or Why Not?

- Change Management discussions

The communication plan provides the team with a consistent opportunity to evolve and improve the execution details behind the Customer Life Cycle model and also to determine when and how to pivot on the strategy.

The Next Phase Plan

As discussed earlier a Customer Life Cycle model is an iterative execution plan. Therefore, the Customer Experience Team will always be planning the next phase of evolution as the company grows.

Using the Gap Analysis from the Design stage, the CX team will evaluate the next set of priorities for implementation and put a project plan together with assignments and timeline for the next phase of the CX implementation. The CX team should review and approve the plan. This plan will become the key set of deliverables for the appropriate organizations to focus on for the next quarter.

The team will plan from quarter to quarter modifying the plan as required in order to continue delivering on the company goals and objectives following the strategic plan for evolving the Customer Life Cycle.

As your organization matures in their CX model, the evolution of the teams will enable them to become more innovative in their abilities to find cost effective ways to better serve the customer and provide more value consistently.

The CX team should remain intact and meet on a frequency that allows the functional areas to continue to collaborate and innovate within each Customer Life Cycle section. This will keep the company focused on being Customer Centric and make this the new corporate way of life.

CHAPTER TEN

Key Concepts to Take Away

To build a successful working CX model requires an entire company dedicated to customer success as a way of life. Theories are great to understand what you want and need to accomplish as a company with a CX model. However, at some point you have to dig in and turn an attractive theory into an executable plan.

The company must buy into the CX model as a companywide commitment. It doesn't work to just create a customer success team in the hope that they can make all things possible for a customer to succeed. A customer's success takes a company commitment from the start of the first customer touch point with your company through every individual interaction they experience during their long term partnership with your company. To achieve this successful result, all organizations within the company should commit to a customer-centric corporate climate change. They need to understand exactly how their contribution creates the right customer perception from an engaging first impression all the way to becoming a long-term loyal customer who refers your company to all their colleagues.

Once your company's leadership team invests in the idea of operating in a customer centric way of life, you will need a vision and a plan. The Customer Life Cycle creates the vision and the high level plan for the organizations to understand precisely how their role, responsibility, and accountability contributes to the delivery of the customer's success.

The company then needs to create a customer experience team, which will lead the development of journey maps for each section of the Customer Life Cycle. These journey maps will help create the detailed executable plan for each organization to begin executing this new way of life for the long-term. These plans will continue to evolve over time following the maturity model. The better your company becomes in executing, modifying and innovating their product, programs, standards, processes, procedures, offerings, etc. the better their ability will be to deliver a consistent, quality, and engaged customer experience where your solution becomes indispensable.

The customer will become a true partner as they embed your solution into their business way of life, evolving along the maturity model roadmap with your solution at the heart of their innovation capability.

Additional Series of Books to follow:

1. A Profitable Services Model within your Customer Experience model

2. A Programmatic approach to Customer Delivery with a Custom feel

3. Build a team passionate about Customer Success

4. Customer Success Programs

ACKNOWLEDGEMENTS

This book has been a work in progress for the last 20 years in the high tech industry. With each software company for whom I worked, I focused on the customer with a philosophy of *"Take care of the customer and the numbers will follow"*.

With this philosophy as my core methodology, I learned a tremendous amount by taking the time to understand each client's business, corporate climate, the team members, and their real problems. I truly became a student that listened and learned from every customer. I must thank the hundreds of customers with whom I had the privilege of working over the years and who taught me so much about what was really important in building a long term partnership and real value.

I am grateful for the mentors throughout my career that believed in my passion to make a real impact on customers and their businesses and spent the time to nurture my abilities, knowledge and leadership skills to help me become a leader that made a difference.

Special thanks to Scott Maxwell, who encouraged me to turn my models and successful approach into workshops and an easy to follow program. He believed in the value I had to offer other companies and he inspired me to write a book that would be interesting and compelling for any growth company. His words of faith and support led me to spend the time to articulate this systematic approach into an easy to follow roadmap.

The talented Ray Goudey did the graphic design on the cover from Ray Goudey Illustrations. I thank him for spending the time to help me create the right graphic for the cover to portray the real key concept of the book, which is to serve your customers at every aspect of their life cycle to equip them to be successful.

Finally, I thank Gerald Golden, my son, who helped me to create the design of the book cover as well as the illustrations and diagrams throughout the book. His creativity and genius in marketing was crucial to the success of the book.

25783422R10077

Made in the USA
Middletown, DE
10 November 2015